ASK PAMELA
Q&A

THE AUSTRALIAN
Women's Weekly

ASK PAMELA
Q&A

PAMELA CLARK ANSWERS ALL
YOUR COOKING QUESTIONS

acp
books

CONTENTS

INTRODUC

Not a day goes by that someone doesn't ask my advice about a recipe, a cooking query, or some problem related to the kitchen. I've been interested in this for more than 30 years, so, inevitably, I've built up quite a memory bank of helpful hints and tips. Here, in this easy-to-use book, are as many questions and answers as I could fit into the given number of pages. Baking, particularly cakes, biscuits, pastry and desserts, seem to cause the

TION

most difficulties, so there are a lot of questions about that, as well as jam making and the correct storage of food (we have included up-to-date information and charts covering this subject).

This is a basic reference book that will become a useful tool in your kitchen because a lot of the old skills are being lost – grandmothers and mothers simply don't have time to pass on information, recipes and techniques to the next generation.

Pamela Clark

Director
The Australian Women's Weekly Test Kitchen

BAKING

Baking powder & bicarbonate of soda

Is it plain or self-raising flour?

Common cake problems solved

Foolproof yeast cooking

Successful pavlovas

Using chocolate with confidence

WHAT IS BAKING POWDER?

Baking powder is a raising agent consisting mainly of two parts cream of tartar (an acid) to one part bicarbonate of soda (an alkaline, also known as baking soda). The acid and alkaline combination, when moistened and heated, gives off carbon dioxide, which aerates and lightens a mixture during baking.

DOES BAKING POWDER HAVE A LIMITED SHELF LIFE?

Once opened, baking powder has a shelf life of up to six months, so always check the use-by-date before buying baking powder. Baking powder begins to lose its ability to leaven (rise) baked goods when it absorbs moisture, so store it in an airtight container in a cool dry place.

IS CARB SODA THE SAME AS BI-CARB SODA?

Yes. The correct name is bicarbonate of soda. It's also known as baking soda in American recipes.

WHAT IS THE DIFFERENCE BETWEEN WHEATEN CORNFLOUR AND CORN (MAIZE) CORNFLOUR?

Cornflour, also known as cornstarch in the U.S., can be made from either wheat (labelled as wheaten cornflour) or corn (maize). Wheaten cornflour has marginally more gluten in it – which helps to form a crust on baked goods such as cakes, biscuits, muffins, etc. They can generally be substituted for each other, the results will be only slightly different. People who have a gluten intolerance should use 100% corn (maize) cornflour.

IS THERE A WAY YOU CAN TELL THE DIFFERENCE BETWEEN PLAIN FLOUR AND SELF-RAISING FLOUR?

To test whether flour is plain or self-raising, place a little on your tongue. If you feel a slight tingle, this indicates that it is self-raising flour; the tingle comes from the bicarbonate of soda. If still in doubt, mix about ¼ cup of the flour to a soft sticky dough with water. Drop the dough into a small saucepan of boiling water. The dough will almost double in size if it's been made using self-raising flour. If it's been made from plain flour it won't expand in size at all.

HOW CAN I TURN PLAIN FLOUR INTO SELF-RAISING FLOUR?

The following proportions are equal to 1 cup of self-raising flour:
1 cup plain flour + 2 teaspoons baking powder, or
1 cup plain flour + 1 teaspoon cream of tartar
+ ½ teaspoon bicarbonate of soda.

I HAVE AN OLD COOKBOOK FOR CAKES, BISCUITS AND DESSERTS, AND THE RECIPES JUST ASK FOR FLOUR. IS THAT SELF-RAISING OR PLAIN FLOUR?

If it does not specify plain or self-raising flour, it is almost certainly plain flour.

WHAT IS THE DIFFERENCE BETWEEN GROUND RICE AND RICE FLOUR?

Ground rice is coarser in texture than rice flour, but they are interchangeable.

WHEN A RECIPE CALLS FOR GROUND ALMONDS OR HAZELNUTS WHAT CAN I USE AS A SUBSTITUTE?

Regrettably, there is no substitute for ground almond or hazelnut (also known as meal) that gives the same moistness and rich, nutty taste. You could try substituting desiccated coconut in recipes where it is used in small quantities but, unfortunately, you can't do this in recipes where it is used in larger quantities.

IS THERE A RULE FOR REPLACING WHITE FLOUR WITH WHOLEMEAL FLOUR IN RECIPES? HOW MUCH EXTRA LIQUID IS REQUIRED?

Use half and half (to start with), white to wholemeal, you might have to add a little more liquid. However, there is no magic formula for substitution. You can increase the wholemeal flour as your family gets used to it, but so much depends on the textures that you like in cakes, cookies, breads, etc. You will just have to experiment to find the proportion that suits you best.

IF YOU WANT TO REPLACE SUGAR WITH HONEY IN RECIPES, IS IT AS SIMPLE AS USING THE SAME AMOUNT OF HONEY INSTEAD OF SUGAR?

Unfortunately not. The results would be quite different as there is less stability in honey than in sugar. As a general rule, don't substitute honey for sugar.

CAN YOU PLEASE TELL ME WHAT MUSCOVADO SUGAR IS AND IF THERE IS AN ALTERNATIVE?

Muscovado sugar (or muscato sugar) is a fine-grained, moist sugar that comes in two types: light and dark.

Light muscovado has a light toffee flavour and is good for sticky toffee sauce. Dark muscovado is used in sweet and spicy sauces.

You could substitute dark brown sugar for muscovado. You should be able to locate it at the supermarket, but if not, try a specialist food store.

I CAME ACROSS AN INTERESTING RECIPE RECENTLY THAT USED GOLDEN CASTER SUGAR. COULD YOU PLEASE TELL ME WHAT IT IS AND WHERE IT IS AVAILABLE?

Golden caster sugar, as it is known in the UK, or raw caster sugar in Australia, is a fine raw sugar that's ideal for cooking as it dissolves more quickly. Its golden colour is great in meringues, biscuits, cakes and desserts, and the subtle presence of molasses adds a delicate flavour.

Raw caster sugar can also be used in place of regular white caster sugar where the finished colour of your baking or dessert isn't important.

Australian raw caster sugar is available in larger supermarkets and imported golden caster sugar is available from specialist food stores.

WHAT'S THE DIFFERENCE BETWEEN ICING SUGAR MIXTURE AND PURE ICING SUGAR?

Icing sugar mixture, also known as confectioners' sugar or powdered sugar, is pulverised granulated sugar that contains a small amount of cornflour (about 3 per cent). Pure icing sugar (confusingly, is also known as confectioners' sugar or powdered sugar) is also made from pulverised granulated sugar but has no added cornflour; it requires a lot of fine sifting as it hardens with age. Pure icing sugar is a must when making royal icing and modelling fondant for cake decorating.

WHAT IS POWDERED SUGAR?

Powdered sugar is simply icing sugar.

IS THERE A SUBSTITUTE FOR CORN SYRUP?

A good substitute for corn syrup is glucose syrup (also known as liquid glucose). It is available in supermarkets, delicatessens, health-food stores and cake decorating suppliers.

CAN I SUBSTITUTE OIL FOR BUTTER OR COOKING MARGARINE?

Sorry, the short answer is "no". The longer answer is, you really have to know what you're doing when substituting ingredients for cooking margarine or butter, so you'd have to be prepared to experiment.

WHENEVER I ADD EGGS TO A "CREAMED" BUTTER AND SUGAR MIXTURE IT ALWAYS CURDLES. I HAVE TRIED CREAMING WITH A WOODEN SPOON AND WITH AN ELECTRIC MIXER, BUT THE RESULT IS ALWAYS THE SAME. I AM CAREFUL TO ADD THE EGGS ONE AT A TIME AND MIX WELL BETWEEN EACH ONE. WHAT AM I DOING WRONG?

There are only two reasons why "creamed" mixtures curdle. The first is the proportion of eggs to the butter/sugar mixture is too high, and no matter what you do, the mix will split or curdle. Sometimes the curdling doesn't matter; the recipe might need a high proportion of eggs for one reason or another, and the mixture will come together later on.

The second is incorrect mixing. Here's the best way to do it, it might take you a few minutes longer, but the results are worth it. Have all the ingredients at room temperature, particularly the butter and eggs, and the milk, too, but it's not as important. Use an electric mixer (it doesn't matter what type, although you tend to under-beat with a hand-held mixer) and, most importantly, use a smallish bowl, this is to help build up the volume of the mixture.

If your kitchen is cold, heat the bowl and the beaters under hot water, then dry them – this makes the butter easier to cream. Beat the butter (butter is best) until it's as white as possible, then add the sugar (if using white sugar, caster sugar is best) all at once. Beat the mixture until it looks light and fluffy; don't try to dissolve the sugar, there is no real need for long beating at this stage, the creaming of the butter is more important. Now, add the eggs, one at a time, and beat the mixture on medium speed *only* until the egg has been absorbed (no need to beat more than that), then add the next egg and so on. The quicker you get the eggs into the butter/sugar mixture, the less chance there is of curdling the cake mixture.

I HAVE TROUBLE WITH ICING ON CAKES. HOW DO I GET IT TO STAY ON? IT ALWAYS FALLS OFF WHEN THE CAKE IS CUT, PARTICULARLY IF THE CAKE HAS BEEN FROZEN.

If you're talking about a glacé (warm) icing, it will almost always fall off the cake when it's cut after freezing. However, you should have more success with butter-based frostings, such as vienna or butter cream or cream-cheese frosting.

CAN ESSENCE BE SUBSTITUTED FOR GRATED CITRUS FRUIT RIND? IF SO, HOW MUCH IS USED?

Essence may be substituted for citrus rind: for every 1 teaspoon of rind required, use about ½ teaspoon of essence – depending on its strength.

CAN I USE A SUBSTITUTE FOR SOUR CREAM IN A CAKE RECIPE?

Depending on what you are making, both yogurt and buttermilk are usually good substitutes for sour cream. When substituting ingredients, the main rule to abide by is that it's okay to substitute in recipes where the ingredient is used in small quantities, but where it is used in larger quantities you run the risk of failure.

WHEN I HAVE LINED A CAKE PAN WITH BAKING PAPER, DO I NEED TO GREASE THE PAPER?

Grease the sides of the pan then line with the paper; this simply holds the paper in place. In most cases, it is not necessary to grease baking paper.

WHAT IS THE BEST THING TO USE TO GREASE A CAKE PAN?

To grease a cake pan, use either a light, even coating of cooking-oil spray, or use a pastry brush to brush melted butter lightly and evenly over the base and sides of the pan.

To grease and flour a cake pan, grease with melted butter and allow it to set before sprinkling with a little flour. Tap the pan, upside-down, on the bench to remove any excess flour from the pan.

WHAT'S THE BEST WAY TO COOL A CAKE?

Stand the cake for up to 15 minutes before turning it onto a wire rack to cool further. Turn the cake, upside-down, onto a wire rack, then turn the cake top-side up immediately using a second rack (unless directed otherwise). Some wire racks can mark a cake, particularly a soft one such as a sponge; to prevent this, cover the rack with baking paper.

If the cake is to be cooled in the pan, it is always covered, and will usually be a fruit cake.

I HAVE TRIED BAKING MUD CAKES, BUT THEY DON'T SEEM TO COOK IN THE MIDDLE. WHAT'S WRONG?

If your mud cake isn't cooking in the middle, it needs longer baking. Often oven temperatures aren't too accurate at the lower temperatures; the longer slower baking won't hurt the cake.

WHAT IS A BUNDT PAN?

A bundt pan is a heavily decorated large ring pan. You can buy them from cookware shops. Grease the pan well before adding the mixture. If you don't have a bundt pan, the cake mixture can usually be baked in two 20cm ring or baba pans.

WHY DOES MY LOAF CAKE ALWAYS SPLIT DURING BAKING?

Most loaf or bar-shaped cakes split during baking, either down the centre or down one long side, or sometimes even down both long sides. This is normal, and is due to the narrow confines of the loaf pan.

I HAVE BEEN UNABLE TO BUY NUT ROLL TINS. WHAT CAN I USE INSTEAD?

They are available in cookware shops and some homeware shops, however, you can make your own nut roll tins from tall 850ml (8cm x 17cm) fruit juice cans. Remove one end from each can by using a can opener that cuts just below the rim. Wash and dry the cans thoroughly before greasing well.

When ready to bake, stand the cans upright on an oven tray, make sure there is enough head room in the oven for the tall cans. Cover the tops of the cans with a piece of strong foil (use a doubled piece if the foil is thin) and secure it with kitchen string. Slash a hole in the foil top to allow the steam to escape during baking.

CAN I BAKE ANY TYPE OF CAKE IN ANY TYPE OF CAKE PAN I LIKE?

There's a lot to know and tell about this, and there is no magic formula.

Some cake mixtures will bake best in a flat open pan. This mostly applies to wet pourable mixtures like mud cakes and gingerbread-type cakes, etc. If these mixtures are baked in deep pans, they often rise and fall in the middle, or they take a long time to cook through.

Butter cakes are usually fairly forgiving and will happily bake in flat, deep or patty pans. The baking times will change, and sometimes the oven temperatures will need to be adjusted slightly, too.

Fruit cakes are really only fruit-packed butter cakes, and can be baked in just about any cake pan you choose – from really large to really small. Baking times and oven temperatures need to be adjusted. Also, the longer a rich fruit cake is baked the darker it becomes – small cakes remain quite (often disappointingly) pale.

I HAVE JUST STARTED BAKING AND AM CONFUSED BY THE MANY BAKING PANS AVAILABLE. WHAT KIND OF BAKING PANS PROVIDE THE BEST RESULTS?

Cake pans are made from many different materials. Here are a few tips on each.

• Aluminium (without non-stick coating) gives the best results, but these are becoming increasingly difficult to find.

• Stainless-steel or tin provides better results if the oven temperature is reduced by 10°C. These tins usually have straight sides and sharp corners. Tin will rust, so dry thoroughly (do this using the oven's stored heat) after washing.

• Non-stick pans are readily available now. Reduce the oven temperature by 10°C as the dark surface absorbs the heat and can cause the cake to burn. Even though the pans are non-stick, we recommend that you grease them lightly or spray them with a cooking-oil spray.

• Silicon bakeware is becoming increasingly popular; buy the best you can afford, and it will last you a lifetime. It does not brown as well as metal but is wonderfully non-stick and flexible, so you can twist it to "pop" the cakes out. Depending on its shape, silicone bakeware, once filled, may need to be supported on an oven tray.

WHAT BASIC CAKE PANS DO YOU RECOMMEND TO START A CAKE PAN COLLECTION?

You should start off your collection with a pan for slices, two loaf pans, a deep 20cm-round pan and at least two oven trays with short sides – no more than 1cm high. A pan for a Christmas cake is also a must – either a deep 19cm- or 20cm-square pan or a deep 22cm- or 23cm-round pan. After buying these pans, add to the collection as you need them. Buy the best quality pans you can, and look after them properly.

I'VE COME ACROSS A FEW RECIPES IN AN OLD COOKBOOK THAT ASK FOR THE CAKE MIXTURE TO BE BAKED IN SANDWICH PANS. WHAT ARE THESE, AND ARE THEY STILL AVAILABLE, OR CAN I USE AN ALTERNATIVE CAKE PAN?

Round sandwich pans were available in 20cm and 23cm sizes, and were always sold in pairs. They were used for making a sponge sandwich and many other types of layered cakes. We were never fans of the sandwich pans, as the cakes baked in them were usually too crusty on top. Use deep pans of the same diameter instead of the now obsolete sandwich pans. The higher-sided pans will give a better result.

RECIPES OFTEN ADVISE TO LINE THE CAKE PAN WITH BAKING PAPER. IS THIS NECESSARY?

Lining a pan with baking paper often provides more than one function, including aiding removal of the cake from the pan; stopping the cake from sticking to the pan and stopping it from burning during long baking times.

BUTTER CAKE PROBLEMS

SINKS IN THE CENTRE AFTER BAKING

This generally means the cake is undercooked.

SINKS IN THE CENTRE WHILE STILL BAKING

Mixture is forced to rise too quickly because the oven is too hot.

CAKE HAS A SUGARY CRUST

The butter and sugar have probably not been creamed sufficiently, or excess sugar was used.

WHITE SPECKS ON TOP

The sugar has not been dissolved enough. It is best to use caster sugar, which dissolves easily during baking. The mixture may not have been creamed sufficiently.

COLOURED STREAKS ON TOP

Ingredients have not been mixed together enough. Bowl scrapings have not been mixed thoroughly into the cake mixture in the pan.

PALE ON TOP

This is caused by using a too-deep pan or having the lining paper too high around the sides of the pan.

EXCESSIVE SHRINKING OF CAKE

The cake was baked at too high a temperature for too long.

JUST HOW SOFT DOES THE BUTTER NEED TO BE FOR CAKE MAKING?

Butter should be soft, but not melted, for cake making. Have butter at room temperature before chopping it into an appropriate-sized bowl. If the kitchen is cold, stand the bowl in warm water for a while. If you forget to take the butter out of the fridge, coarsely grate it into the mixing bowl.

BUTTER CAKE PROBLEMS

CAKE CRUMBLES WHEN CUT

Mixture may have been creamed too much, particularly in cakes containing fruit.

CAKE STICKS TO PAN

Too much sugar or other sweetening in the recipe. If a recipe contains honey or golden syrup, or if you're using a new pan, it is wise to grease the pan then line it with baking paper.

COLLAR AROUND TOP OUTSIDE EDGE

Cake was probably baked at too high a temperature.

CAKE RISES AND CRACKS IN THE CENTRE

This is caused by using a cake pan that is too small; most cakes baked in loaf, bar or ring pans crack slightly due to the confined space of the pan. Also, the oven may have been too hot.

UNEVEN RISING

The oven shelf has not been set straight or the oven is not level on the floor. The mixture has not been spread evenly into the pan.

HOLES IN BAKED CAKE

This occurs if the mixture has not been creamed sufficiently. The oven may have been too hot.

WHAT IS THE BEST PAN TO USE WHEN MAKING SPONGE CAKES?

Deep-sided pans give the best results as the high sides protect the delicate sponge mixture and prevents a crisp crust developing. Aluminium pans are best. Cake pans made from tin, or are anodised or coated with a non-stick surface, cook more rapidly, so it is wise to lower the oven temperature by 10°C. Unless recipes state otherwise, a light but even greasing using a pastry brush dipped in melted butter will give the best results.

When dividing a sponge mixture between the pans, gently spread the mixture to the edge of the pans as the mixture will not spread in the heat of the oven. The last scrapings from the bowl in which the sponge was mixed should be placed around the edge of the mixture in the pans; this is the heaviest part of the mixture and if it's placed in the centre of the sponge it will make a dark heavy patch in the centre. To break large air bubbles, run a knife through the sponge mixture several times or tap the sponge pans, once, firmly on the bench.

CAN I BAKE TWO SPONGE CAKES AT A TIME IN THE OVEN?

Fan-forced ovens should bake the sponges evenly, regardless of where they are in the oven. However, some ovens bake unevenly, so you need to reposition the sponges to get even baking and browning.

If the sponges are being baked on different shelves, it will be necessary to swap them around after half the baking time has passed, to make sure the cakes bake evenly. If the sponges are being baked on the same shelf, the one towards the back of the oven needs to come forward after half the baking time to ensure even baking.

The cakes won't be adversely affected if you move fairly quickly and handle the pans carefully after half the baking time has expired. Opening the oven door does decrease the temperature and can affect the cake's rising if you do it during the early stages of baking.

HOW DO YOU KNOW WHEN A SPONGE CAKE IS COOKED?

When baked, the sponge will be just beginning to shrink from the side of the pan and it should feel slightly springy to the touch. Turn sponges out immediately; if you leave them in the pan, they will continue to bake, shrink and dry out. Turn onto a wire rack, then immediately turn right-side up onto a baking-paper-lined rack to prevent the wire racks from marking the tops.

WHY DOES MY SPONGE CAKE HAVE A MERINGUE-LIKE CRUST ON IT WHEN COOKED?

This crust is caused by undissolved sugar. Use the finer caster sugar, not regular table sugar, and make sure every grain is dissolved before adding flour, liquid etc. The process of dissolving sugar usually takes about 10 minutes in a deep-sided bowl, using a mixer on a stand; people tend to give up too early in the mixing if they're using a hand-held mixer.

HOW DO YOU STOP CRUMBS FROM STICKING TO THE ICING WHEN ICING A SPONGE CAKE?

Put the cake to be iced in the freezer until it's really cold, but not frozen – the time this will take will depend on your freezer. This will certainly help prevent crumbs getting mixed up with the icing.

MY SPONGE CAKES ALWAYS RISE QUICKLY IN THE OVEN, BUT THEN SHRINK. WHY?

This is usually due to baking at too high an oven temperature. Make sure the oven temperature is set correctly, especially if using a fan-forced oven.

SPONGE CAKE PROBLEMS

STREAKS ON TOP OF CAKE

Scrapings from the mixing bowl were not mixed into the sponge mixture; scrapings are always slightly darker than the rest of the mixture. It is best to put scrapings from the mixing bowl towards the side of the pan – not in the centre.

SMALL WHITE SPECKS ON TOP

Caused by undissolved sugar; sugar should be added gradually to the eggs and beaten until completely dissolved between additions.

PALE AND STICKY ON TOP

Baking at too low an oven temperature, or wrong oven position.

CRUSTY ON TOP

Baking at too high an oven temperature, or wrong oven position or pan was too small. Using high-sided cake pans protects the cake mixture.

SHRINKS IN OVEN

The cake was baked at too high a temperature or for too long.

WRINKLES DURING COOLING

Insufficient baking time, or the cake was cooled in a draughty area.

FLAT AND TOUGH

Incorrect folding in of flour and liquid. The flour should be triple-sifted and folded into the mixture in a gentle, circular motion.

SINKS IN THE CENTRE

The pan was too small, causing the cake to rise quickly, then fall in the centre.

IS UNDERCOOKED

Oven door may have been opened during first half of the baking time.

WHY DO MY PAVLOVAS CRACK? THE TOP STAYS RISEN WITH A BIG AIRSPACE BETWEEN IT AND THE MARSHMALLOW BUT IT ALL BREAKS AWAY WHEN IT IS FILLED.

This is just what domestically-made pavlovas do, especially in humid or wet weather when the meringue crust absorbs moisture from the air. Always add the cream to the pavlova as late as possible; just before serving is best.

WHEN MAKING PAVLOVA, I GET BITS OF SHELL AND SPECKS OF YOLK IN MY EGG WHITES. CAN I SALVAGE THE WHITES?

Egg whites won't whip if they come into contact with any fat, so it's important to make sure you don't end up with any yolk in the egg whites when you separate them. If you do, you can usually scoop out the scrap of yolk by dipping the shell into the whites – this is also the best way to extricate any shell that might end up in the bowl during separation.

WHAT RATIO OF SUGAR TO EGG WHITES SHOULD YOU USE TO MAKE MERINGUE OR PAVLOVA?

The classic proportion is ¼ cup (55g) sugar to 1 egg white, but this can be increased or decreased slightly to compensate for the varying sizes of egg whites. It is possible to increase or decrease the classic proportion of sugar to egg white for different results. A higher amount of sugar will give a more crusty, crisp drier meringue, which is good for meringue cases that need to be stored, then filled later. If the meringues are nicely dried out in the oven, they will keep in an airtight container at room temperature for many weeks. A lesser amount of sugar will give a much softer, less crusty meringue – these need to be eaten soon after baking.

WHY DOES MY PAVLOVA WEEP?

This is usually caused by undissolved sugar. Beat the egg whites only until soft peaks form before you start adding the sugar; if you beat the whites until they are stiff and dry, the sugar will take longer to dissolve. If the sugar doesn't dissolve properly the meringue can "weep" droplets of moisture during and after baking.

To make sure the sugar is properly dissolved rub a small quantity of the egg-white mixture between your fingertips; if it feels smooth, the sugar is dissolved, if it's granular you need to keep beating for a while longer.

"Weeping" isn't the end of the world, however, it's just an appearance thing. The pavlova will still taste as yummy, it just mightn't look as good.

WHY DO SOME PAVLOVA RECIPES INCLUDE CORNFLOUR AND VINEGAR AND OTHERS DON'T?

Cornflour and vinegar contribute to the development of marshmallowy centres in pavlovas. However, we don't think the addition of these makes much difference. Some cooks swear by it, others, like us, think the dissolving of the sugar and the baking is far more important. Try both ways; you'll be surprised at the difference – or lack of it.

WHY IS IT THAT EVERY TIME I MAKE A MERINGUE OR PAVLOVA THE RESULTS ARE DIFFERENT?

The weather, particularly wet or humid weather, contributes to the success of pavlovas. Sugar absorbs and holds moisture from the moist air, and this can cause the crust on the baked meringue or pavlova to weep and/or collapse on standing. It's almost impossible to combat this, longer drying out of the meringue or pavlova in the oven is the only way to help fight this problem.

WHEN I TRY TO MAKE BREAD IT IS VERY HEAVY IN THE CENTRE. WHY DOES THIS HAPPEN?

If your loaf is small and heavy, it could be caused by insufficient kneading, stale yeast or dough that is too stiff. Leaving the dough to prove for too long may also cause a heavy loaf.

MY HOMEMADE BREAD IS VERY COARSE IN TEXTURE. WHY IS THIS?

If the bread is coarse in texture, it could be that the dough was too wet, or because it was proved too long, or baked at the wrong temperature.

I HAVE A FEW RECIPES THAT LIST "STRONG FLOUR" AS AN INGREDIENT – WHAT IS THE AUSTRALIAN EQUIVALENT?

Strong flour is produced from a variety of wheat that has a high gluten (protein) content and is best suited for pizza and bread making: the expansion caused by the yeast and the stretchiness caused by kneading require a flour that is "strong" enough to handle these stresses. "Soft", or plain (all-purpose), flour is made from wheat varieties that have a lower protein content, and is used mainly for making cakes and biscuits of a lighter texture. Since domestic electric bread makers entered the marketplace, it is now easier to find strong flour; look for it – sold as strong, gluten-enriched baker's flour or bread-mix flour – at your supermarket or in health-food stores.

WHY DOES MY HOMEMADE BREAD TASTE SO YEASTY?

If the bread tastes too "yeasty", it could be because it was made in hot weather, or the dough was risen in too warm a place, resulting in too quick a rising. Or, it could be that too much yeast was used.

WHAT IS COMPRESSED YEAST?

Compressed yeast, also known as fresh yeast, comes in chunks that look rather like putty-coloured modelling clay. It should be pale and smell slightly and pleasantly of alcohol; dark patches and a strong smell means it is stale and may not work. It crumbles easily, and will keep in an airtight jar in the fridge for about 2 weeks; it can be frozen, but sometimes seems a bit reluctant to work after thawing.

CAN I USE COMPRESSED YEAST INSTEAD OF DRIED?

Yes, compressed and dried yeasts can be substituted for each other. One 7g sachet (3 teaspoons) of dried yeast is equivalent to 15g (3 teaspoons) of compressed or fresh yeast.

WHEN USING YEAST JUST HOW HOT SHOULD THE WATER BE?

Yeast likes warmth, but it takes only 60°C heat to kill it. If you are using compressed yeast, the water should be lukewarm. If you are using dried yeast, the water should be comfortably hand-warm.

CAN I MAKE HOT CROSS BUNS A DAY BEFORE NEEDED?

Homemade hot cross buns have a much stronger yeasty flavour than commercially made buns and they won't keep for more than a day or so. You'll notice hot cross buns appearing in supermarkets weeks before Easter – that's because they have preservatives added. Rather than slaving over the buns on Easter Sunday, make them the day before – put the shaped buns in the pan, then cover them loosely with oiled plastic wrap. Put them in the fridge overnight. They will prove in the fridge. All you have to do the next day is make the crosses, then bake the buns.

I AM MAKING BREAD AND THE RECIPE USES A DOUGH HOOK IN AN ELECTRIC MIXER. CAN I DO THIS BY HAND?

Kneading can be done by hand or with a dough hook. To hand-knead, flour a work surface, place the dough on top (it will be sticky) and continuously fold the dough over towards you and push firmly away with the heel of your hand. Turn the dough a quarter turn after every second kneading. Sprinkle flour over as needed, but be sparing. The dough is sufficiently kneaded when it is smooth and elastic and the impression of a finger, pressed in, quickly disappears. This kneading usually takes about 10 minutes; a dough hook will do the job in about a quarter of the time.

COULD YOU TELL ME WHY MY BREAD DOUGH IS NOT RISING?

Usually, dough won't rise if the yeast has been warmed and activated incorrectly, or the yeast has been killed by too much heat.

Put the dough in a lightly oiled bowl, turn to oil all over, then cover with greased plastic wrap and leave in a warm place until the dough doubles in bulk. You can slow down the rise if it suits you, by leaving the bowl in a cooler place (even in the fridge) overnight; many authorities say a slow rise gives better bread, having a finer crumb and better keeping quality. Bring the dough back to room temperature before proceeding. The dough is sufficiently risen when the impression of two fingers, quickly and lightly pressed in, remains.

HOW CAN I TELL WHEN MY BREAD IS COOKED?

After the baking time has passed, and the bread looks well risen, browned and crusty, remove it from the oven, turn it onto a thick towel and tap the bottom. Properly baked bread will sound hollow.

WHAT IS THE BEST WAY TO MIX SCONE DOUGH?

Use a round-ended table knife to "cut" the liquid through the flour and butter mixture. The finished dough should be soft and sticky, just holding its shape when turned out. Turn the mixture onto a floured work surface, dust your hands with flour and shape the dough into a smooth ball by working it gently into a manageable, smooth shape. Sprinkle with a little more flour if necessary, but be sparing. Flatten the dough with your hand and pat it out into an even 2cm thickness, pressing from the centre outwards. Using a sharp metal cutter dipped in flour each time, cut scones out close together, pushing the cutter sharply down and removing it without twisting. Lightly work the scraps together and press the dough out again, slightly thicker, to cut the remaining scones. The scones from the first cutting will be the lightest.

WHICH IS THE BEST POSITION IN THE OVEN TO BAKE SCONES?

Position the oven rack in the hottest part of the oven, usually the top shelf (scones need to rise quickly to be light). Preheat the oven to its highest temperature. Reduce the heat to the temperature indicated in the recipe just after you've put the scones in the oven.

CAN I BAKE MY SCONES ON AN OVEN TRAY?

Scones can be baked on open, sideless oven trays, but they sometimes fall over, and sometimes brown too much, particularly those on the outer edges of the batch. It's best to cook scones close together in shallow cake pans. This will give you straight-sided scones with crusty tops and bottoms and soft sides. They need to be baked slightly longer than scones on open oven trays. Check them after about 15 minutes; turn the pan around to ensure even browning.

IS IT NECESSARY TO GLAZE SCONES BEFORE BAKING?

Glazing is not necessary, but it removes excess flour from the tops of scones and encourages them to brown. Brush the tops of the scones once they're in the pan or on the oven tray, using a brush dipped in water, milk or egg: water results in a light brown colour, egg gives a golden brown colour, and milk is between the two. Milk and egg also give the tops a sheen. Brush the tops lightly – they should be just damp, not wet.

HOW DO I KNOW WHEN MY SCONES ARE COOKED?

Scones are cooked when they are browned and sound hollow when tapped firmly on top with your fingers. For even crustier scones, turn them onto a wire rack to cool; for softer-topped scones, wrap them in a tea-towel while still hot.

WHY DON'T MY SCONES RISE?

There are a number of reasons why your scones didn't rise. It could be that you may have not added enough liquid to make a soft sticky dough, or over-mixed the scone dough, or used plain flour instead of self-raising by mistake, or the oven may not have been hot enough.

I MADE SCONES USING WHOLEMEAL FLOUR AND THEY TURNED OUT LIKE ROCKS. WHY?

Scones made using all wholemeal flour tend to be heavy. Try using half white and half wholemeal flour; this is a good compromise. You'll need to add a little more liquid than the recipe suggests to compensate for the higher absorbency rate of wholemeal flour. Aim to make a soft sticky dough.

WHEN USING FROZEN BERRIES IN MUFFINS, SHOULD THEY BE THAWED BEFORE USING?

Frozen berries should be used while they are still frozen, this way they keep their shape and don't "bleed" into the mixture too much.

HOW DO I KNOW WHEN MY MUFFINS ARE COOKED?

Muffins should be browned, risen, firm to the touch and beginning to shrink from the sides of the pan when they are cooked. If in doubt, insert a metal skewer into the muffin. It should be clean and free of mixture when it comes out. Turn the muffins onto a wire rack as soon as they are baked to prevent them becoming steamy. The exception to this advice is when the muffins are filled with custard, caramel or jam. In this instance they should stand in the pans to cool for a few minutes before turning out. The fillings can be extremely hot.

CAN I USE A HAND-HELD BEATER TO MIX MUFFINS?

There's no need to use a beater unless the recipe requires you to beat the butter, sugar and eggs until light and fluffly. Muffins are quick and low-fuss to make and mostly require only a single bowl for the mixing.

The butter is usually cubed and firm from the refrigerator when it is rubbed into the dry ingredients, then the flavourings are lightly mixed in and finally the egg and milk or other liquid is added. Muffins toughen if the mixture is overhandled, so the less mixing, the lighter the finished texture. Use a fork or a large metal spoon to cut the liquid through the dry ingredients, and don't worry if the mix seems a bit lumpy – it will be fine when baked.

I WOULD LIKE TO START MAKING BISCUITS AND SLICES. WHAT PANS DO I NEED TO PURCHASE?

The shape of a baking pan or oven tray affects the way biscuits and slices bake. For biscuits, use either flat oven trays or pans with shallow sides so that the heat "skims" over the top and ensures proper circulation and browning.

For slices, use slice or lamington pans. These are rectangular pans, with sides about 2.5cm high.

CAN I BAKE TWO TRAYS OF BISCUITS IN THE OVEN AT ONCE?

Two or more trays or pans of biscuits or slices can be baked in the oven at the same time, provided the pans don't touch the oven sides or the door when it is closed, and each tray should have a 2cm space around it to allow for proper heat circulation.

For even baking, swap the positions of the pans halfway through the baking time. You may also need to turn pans front-to-back to brown biscuits evenly.

As a general rule, the top half of a gas oven is best for baking biscuits, but in an electric oven, the lower half is usually best. Fan-forced ovens should maintain even heat throughout the oven, so you should not have to change the trays around – however, you should check them once or twice.

WHENEVER I ADD SULTANAS OR RAISINS TO BISCUIT DOUGH THEY END UP DRIED AND SHRIVELLED ON TOP. HOW CAN I STOP THIS?

Hydrate the fruit, which will minimise burning; soak the dried sultanas or raisins in a little warm water for about 20 minutes, then drain the fruit well and pat dry before using. Also, after you roll or drop the biscuit mixture onto the tray, gently push any fruit that's sticking out back into the mixture before baking to ensure the fruit doesn't burn.

HOW DO I TEST IF BISCUITS ARE COOKED?

Biscuits generally feel soft in the oven and become firmer as they cool on wire racks. Some of the crisper varieties of biscuits are cooled on the oven trays; follow each recipe's instructions. A good test for most types of biscuits is to push one biscuit on the tray gently with your thumb; if it moves without breaking, the biscuit is cooked.

BISCUIT PROBLEMS

BISCUITS ARE TOO HARD

The ingredients may have been measured incorrectly or the biscuits may have been baked at too high a temperature or for too long.

BISCUITS ARE TOO SOFT

The ingredients may have been measured incorrectly or the biscuits may have been baked at too low a temperature or for not long enough. If biscuits are not cooled as directed, or are stacked on top of each other to cool, they may be softened because the moist heat they give off cannot disperse.

BISCUITS SPREAD TOO MUCH WHILE BAKING

The mixture may have been too soft because of overbeating the butter and sugar (and egg in some cases); the ingredients may have been measured incorrectly; the wrong type of flour may have been used; or the oven may not have been hot enough to set the mixture quickly.

BISCUITS ARE TOO BROWN UNDERNEATH

The trays may have been over-greased; excess greasing will burn and, in turn, burn the biscuits. Incorrect oven position and/or temperature can also cause over-browning, so can over-measuring sweet ingredients.

CAN I MAKE SHORTCRUST PASTRY IN A FOOD PROCESSOR?

You can make good shortcrust pastry in a food processor as long as you are fast on the pulse button. Place the flour and diced cold butter in the bowl of the processor, combine with short bursts of power, then add the water and egg yolk, if using, and mix with just a few very short bursts, stopping immediately the mixture starts to form a ball.

WHAT DOES BAKING BLIND MEAN?

Baking blind means baking or partially baking a pastry case without the filling. Place a circle of baking paper, about 5cm larger than the base of the pastry case, over the pastry and fill with uncooked rice or dried beans to weigh down the pastry so it will not rise. Some recipes will tell you to prick the pastry case all over with a fork, then bake blind – bake as directed in the recipe. Pastry cases, especially small tartlets, are sometimes pricked all over with a fork to help prevent rising, instead of being baked blind.

WHEN MAKING SHORTCRUST PASTRY, WHY DOES IT NEED TO BE REFRIGERATED BEFORE ROLLING?

The dough is wrapped and refrigerated for 30 minutes (or as the recipe directs) so that its moisture content will even out and the gluten (the protein in the flour) will have time to relax, to minimise shrinkage during baking. No harm is done by a longer resting (provided you give the dough time to become pliable before you roll it out); in fact, many cooks think their pastry is more tender if it has had a long rest. After rolling and shaping, rest the pastry again before baking.

COULD YOU GIVE ME SOME TIPS ON HOW TO HANDLE PASTRY?

Kneading means turning the outside edges of the dough into the centre. When applied to most pastries it is not the heavy action you might apply to bread making, just working the dough lightly into a manageable shape.

We find it's best to roll out pastry between sheets of baking or greaseproof paper or plastic wrap. If you work on a floured surface with a floured rolling pin, there's always the risk you'll upset the balance of ingredients by working too much flour into the pastry. Besides, it's easier to pick up a sheet of pastry and transfer it to the pie dish when there's a sheet of paper or plastic supporting it. Start rolling with short light strokes from the centre outwards, each time rolling the pastry towards you then away from you. Reduce the pressure towards the edges and don't roll over the edges. Pastry is best rolled on a cold surface; marble is perfect, but your benchtop will be fine, so long as it's smooth and clean.

WHY DOES PASTRY DOUGH CRACK WHEN ROLLING?

If the dough cracks when you're rolling it out, it may have been chilled too long; allow it to rest for a short period of time. Most commonly, however, the pastry has probably been over-handled. The proteins in the flour (gluten) toughens with over-handling, and will certainly cause the pastry to crack during the rolling process. If you're making pastry in a processor, pulse the ingredients. If you're making the pastry by hand, handle it quickly and lightly.

Be sure to roll the dough evenly and lightly near the edges to help prevent cracking. Small cracks or tears can be fixed by rubbing a little water along the crack then pulling the edges together and pressing the seam to seal it.

WHAT IS THE BEST TYPE OF CHOCOLATE TO USE IN BAKING?

We use eating-quality chocolate rather than cooking chocolate. Avoid using anything labelled compound chocolate, as some of the cocoa butter is replaced with other vegetable fats such as palm, coconut or soya oil, and the result is a waxy tasting chocolate.

Exceptions to this rule are when the recipes call for chocolate Melts or Choc Bits. Chocolate Melts are made from compound chocolate and are sometimes used when chocolate has to be piped or used for dipping. Because of the higher vegetable oil content, melted chocolate Melts don't set as quickly as better quality chocolate. Choc Bits, sometimes specified in cookies or muffins, also contain less cocoa butter than quality chocolate, so will keep their shape when baked.

HOW IS CHOCOLATE BEST STORED?

Chocolate should be stored in cool, dry conditions. If it becomes too warm, the cocoa butter rises to the surface and a whiteish-grey film or "bloom" develops. The chocolate will still taste the same and, once melted, will usually return to its original colour. If chocolate has been refrigerated or frozen, bring it to room temperature before using.

I'VE HEARD THAT YOU CAN USE A PLASTIC BAG TO PIPE CHOCOLATE. HOW IS THIS DONE?

Plastic bags are useful for piping. Place chocolate in a small microwave-safe plastic bag you plan to use as a piping bag. Fold the open end over and tuck underneath the bag to close the opening, then microwave on MEDIUM (75%) for 20-second intervals until chocolate is melted. Use a cloth to rub the bag to ensure chocolate is melting. Cool slightly, then ease the chocolate into one corner of the bag and twist the top of the bag so chocolate is pressed firmly into the corner. Snip a *tiny* bit off the corner of the bag to pipe the chocolate.

HOW DO I MELT CHOCOLATE WITHOUT RUINING IT?

Because all chocolate scorches easily and thus becomes grainy, which ruins the flavour, all care should be taken to melt it slowly, over very low heat. Care must be taken to ensure that when melting chocolate it does not come into contact with water. If it does, it will "seize", that is, become lumpy and lose its sheen. If this occurs, you'll have to begin again with a different piece of chocolate.

For this same reason, never cover chocolate when melting it because the condensation that forms inside the lid will drop beads of moisture into the chocolate.

If you melt chocolate over a pan of water or in a double saucepan, be careful that the bottom of the bowl holding the chocolate does not touch the hot water in the pan, as the heat of the water can cause the chocolate to burn.

Don't melt chocolate in a plastic container because that material is not an even conductor of heat. Use a container made from china or glass, as these conduct heat slowly and will melt the chocolate more evenly. You can use metal bowls, but be aware that the chocolate will melt quickly, so you'll need to watch it carefully.

One of the easiest ways to melt chocolate is to place chopped chocolate in an uncovered microwave-safe container in a microwave oven; microwave on MEDIUM (75%) in 20-second bursts, removing the container the second the chocolate is melted. Some chocolate holds its shape even when melted, so care must be taken to ensure you don't burn it. After the first 20 seconds in the microwave oven, take the chocolate out and gently stir it to see if it has melted. Adjust the cooking time, depending on how soft it is – it may only need another 10 seconds, not 20 seconds, until it has melted sufficiently.

I WOULD LIKE TO TRY MAKING CHOCOLATE CURLS TO DECORATE CAKES. HOW IS THIS DONE?

A very simple way to make small chocolate curls is to scrape the long side of a block of chocolate with a vegetable peeler. However, making curls using melted chocolate is also relatively easy.

Spread melted chocolate evenly over a cold surface – marble is great, but a cold flat oven tray is also fine; put it in the fridge to cool. Leave the chocolate to stand at room temperature until almost set. Drag the blade of a large sharp knife, held at about a 45° angle, across the chocolate to make the curls. It is important that the chocolate is at the right stage. If it hasn't set enough it will not curl, and if it has set too much, it will break.

You could also try scraping a melon baller across the chocolate to make small curls or drag an ice-cream scoop across the chocolate to make larger curls.

I HAVE A RECIPE THAT ASKS FOR COUVERTURE CHOCOLATE. WHAT IS IT?

Couverture (meaning "covering" in French) is a term used to describe a fine quality, very rich chocolate high in both cocoa butter and cocoa liquor. It must have a cocoa butter content of at least 32 per cent. Couverture chocolate must be tempered – heated and cooled to specific temperatures – before being used; this stabilises the cocoa butter. It is a complex process and is usually only done by professionals to achieve a smooth, high-gloss coating, like you see in high quality hand-made chocolates.

Many grades of good eating-quality chocolate are available, and can be substituted for couverture chocolate, however the results will be different. Dark eating chocolate, also known as semi-sweet or luxury chocolate, is a good substitute, as it is made with a high percentage of cocoa liquor and cocoa butter, and a little sugar, and doesn't need tempering. Don't substitute with dark compound cooking chocolate, which is made using vegetable oils.

CHRISTMAS

Solve Christmas cake problems

Reheating Christmas puddings

Get crispy crackle on roast pork

Cooking whole salmon

Carving the turkey & ham

I HAVE JUST MADE MINI FRUIT CAKES AND THEY ARE VERY DRY. WHAT CAN I DO TO FIX THIS?

Warm the cakes through by wrapping them in foil and putting them in a slow oven (150°C/130°C fan-forced) for 30 minutes. While they're warming, make a sugar syrup using equal quantities of sugar and alcohol (sherry is inexpensive and works well). Bring the ingredients to the boil, remove from the heat, then pour the hot syrup slowly over the warmed cakes. Each cake should absorb about ⅓ cup, maybe more. This should save them for you.

I HAVE JUST CUT THE TOP OFF MY CHRISTMAS CAKE TO FIND THAT IT LOOKS AS IF IT HAS NOT COOKED ALL THE WAY THROUGH. CAN I PUT IT BACK IN THE OVEN?

Try slicing off the cooked outside parts of the cake, then wrap the uncooked part in foil, and heat it through in a slow oven (150°/130°C fan-forced). We can't guess at how long it would take to dry out, maybe an hour, just keep checking. Alternatively, you could heat it through and hopefully cook it some more over steam, as you would a pudding. If you reheat the whole cake, you run the risk of drying out the already cooked sections.

CAN I REHEAT A STEAMED CHRISTMAS PUDDING IN THE MICROWAVE OVEN?

Yes. To reheat a whole, large pudding, cover it with microwave-safe plastic wrap, then microwave on MEDIUM (50%) for about 15 minutes. To reheat a single serving, cover the slice with microwave-safe plastic wrap and microwave on HIGH (100%) for 30 to 60 seconds. These times are only a guide; you should check the oven manufacturer's instructions.

IF I SUBSTITUTE FRUIT JUICE FOR ALCOHOL IN A FRUIT CAKE RECIPE WILL IT KEEP FOR THE SAME AMOUNT OF TIME (6 MONTHS)?

Yes. Actually, it's the sugar and the natural sugars in the dried fruit that preserves cakes and puddings, not the alcohol.

I HAVE MADE A BOILED PINEAPPLE RUM CAKE. SHOULD IT BE KEPT IN THE REFRIGERATOR BECAUSE IT CONTAINS PINEAPPLE?

Keep the cake in the fridge during wet or humid weather as it is a moist cake and can develop mould easily. It will also cut better when it's fridge-cold.

I WANT TO MAKE SMALL FRUIT CAKES FOR CHRISTMAS IN A TEXAS MUFFIN PAN. HOW LONG WILL I NEED TO COOK THEM?

They will take about 1 hour in a very slow oven (120°C/100°C fan-forced); they need as long as possible in the oven to darken the cake mixture.

HOW DO I REHEAT A BOILED PUDDING ON CHRISTMAS DAY?

If the pudding is frozen, thaw it for three days in the refrigerator. Remove it from the refrigerator 12 hours before reheating.

Tie a dry unfloured cloth around the pudding. Boil, covered, for 2 hours in a large boiler about three-quarters filled with boiling water. Hang the hot pudding for 10 minutes before removing the cloth, then stand for at least 20 minutes before serving.

HOW FAR IN ADVANCE CAN I MAKE A BOILED CHRISTMAS PUDDING?

After removing the cloth, allow the pudding to come to room temperature then wrap it in plastic wrap and seal tightly in a freezer bag or airtight container. A boiled Christmas pudding can be refrigerated for three months or frozen for up to one year.

CHRISTMAS CAKE PROBLEMS

FRUIT SINKS TO THE BOTTOM

A number of things may cause the fruit to sink to the bottom of the cake, including the fruit not being dried thoroughly if it has been washed; self-raising flour may have been used instead of plain flour; or the cake mixture is too soft to support the weight of the fruit (caused by over-creaming). The fruit should be finely chopped to about the size of a sultana so the mixture can support it.

DOUGHY IN THE CENTRE

The cake is baked in too cool an oven, or for not long enough.

BURNT BOTTOM ON CAKE

The cake was wrongly positioned in the oven or the pans were lined incorrectly, or the cake was baked at too high a temperature. Rich fruit cakes require protection during long, slow baking times. Cakes that are 22cm or smaller require three thicknesses of baking-paper lining; larger cakes need one or two sheets of brown paper and three sheets of baking paper.

UNEVEN RISING

The oven shelf or the oven is not level, or the mixture was spread unevenly in the pan; use a wet spatula to level the top of the cake mixture.

HOW FAR IN ADVANCE CAN I MAKE A STEAMED CHRISTMAS PUDDING?

The pudding can be made up to three months ahead and kept refrigerated, or made up to one year ahead and frozen. If the pudding was made in an aluminium steamer, remove the pudding from the steamer and wrap in plastic wrap before storing.

CHRISTMAS CAKE PROBLEMS

CREAMED MIXTURE CURDLES

Eggs and butter were not at room temperature or the eggs were not added quickly enough to the creamed butter and sugar mixture. Eggs may be too large for the mixture to absorb the excess liquid. If the eggs used are larger than 60g in weight, omit one of the number shown in the ingredients list, or add only the yolk of one of the eggs. A curdled creamed mixture could cause the finished cake to crumble when cut.

SINKS IN THE MIDDLE

Self-raising flour may have been used, or too much bicarbonate of soda was added. (Usually only plain flour is used in rich fruit cakes, but sometimes a small portion of self-raising flour is added to the mixture.) The cake may not have been baked properly. To test if the cake is cooked, push a sharp-pointed knife (a vegetable knife is good), rather than a skewer, through the centre to the base of the pan; the size of the knife blade surface helps distinguish between uncooked mixture or fruit and cooked mixture. Test only after the minimum specified baking time.

CRACKS ON TOP

Cake was cooked at too high a temperature.

WHAT IS THE DIFFERENCE IN USING FRESH SUET, PACKAGED SUET MIX OR BUTTER IN A CHRISTMAS PUDDING?

Suet is a very hard fat, which melts slowly through a mixture during the cooking, whereas butter melts very easily and quickly through a mixture. They are different types of fats and shouldn't be substituted for each other. The packaged suet has a lot of starches added to it, and is quite different from fresh suet. You need to order fresh suet from a butcher (order double the amount to end up with the quantity the recipe specifies). Remove all the connective tissue, grate the suet finely, then rub it into the flour with your fingertips.

I WOULD LIKE TO MAKE FRUIT MINCE PIES FOR CHRISTMAS – CAN I MAKE THE FRUIT MINCE IN ADVANCE?

Fruit mince can be made many months in advance – store it in a cool dark place, in an airtight container, the refrigerator is the safest place. There are many different fruit mince recipes around, however, if the recipe contains nuts, be aware that there is always the danger of nuts turning rancid, particularly in warm climates.

HOW FAR IN ADVANCE CAN I MAKE A GINGERBREAD HOUSE?

The gingerbread pieces for the house can be made up to a month ahead if the weather remains dry. It's important to cook the gingerbread until it's crisp. Store the gingerbread in an airtight container with as little air space left in the container as possible.

Assemble the gingerbread house as close to serving as possible. If the house is to be used as a centrepiece for the table, keep the house away from the dust and insects. If the house is a gift, wrap it in cellophane to keep it as airtight and dust-free as possible.

I AM BAKING A 4KG ROAST PORK FOR CHRISTMAS DAY. HOW LONG WILL IT TAKE TO COOK?

Allow 30 minutes per 500g if the roast is over 3kg, 40 minutes per 1kg if the roast is under 3kg. If you have a meat thermometer, use it to check the meat is done – insert the thermometer into the centre of the thickest part of the joint, away from any bone, fat and gristle – the roast is cooked when the temperature reaches 71°C to 76°C.

If you don't have a meat thermometer, check the doneness by inserting a fine skewer into the centre towards the end of the cooking time. If the skewer goes in easily and the juices that run out are clear, the meat is done.

Rest a cooked roast, wrapped or covered tightly in foil, for 15 minutes before carving. This allows the juices to settle into the meat.

HOW DO I GET THE RIND ON MY ROAST PORK TO CRISP PROPERLY?

The rind on a roast provides one of pork's greatest joys: crisp and bubbly crackling. Have the rind scored by the butcher, or do it yourself by cutting through the rind into the underlying fat at 1cm intervals. Stand the roast on a rack in the sink and pour about 2 cups of boiling water over the rind, then rub the rind with oil and coarse cooking salt. Cook the roast in a preheated oven at the highest heat for 20 minutes or until the skin bubbles, then reduce the oven temperature to moderate (180°C/160°C fan-forced) and continue cooking. Don't baste, cover or turn roasts that have crackling. The initial 20 minutes is included in the total cooking time.

Rest the roast covered *loosely* with foil (to stop softening the crackling) for about 15 minutes. Or, alternatively, carefully remove the crackling from the roast to an oven tray, return it to the oven while the roast is resting for 15 minutes covered tightly in foil.

HOW DO YOU CARVE A TURKEY?

Allow the hot turkey to rest, covered, for at least 20 minutes before carving so the juices settle. Remove any skewers or string if you trussed the bird. Carve one side of the bird at a time and only carve enough meat for the meal. Carve the dark meat before the light meat, as dark meat will stay moist longer.

First remove wings, legs and thighs. To remove the wing, hold the free part with one hand and gently pull it away from the body. Cut down between the wing and the breast until you reach the shoulder joint, then cut through the joint, not the bone, and pull the wing away from the bird.

Use a carving fork to steady the turkey; cut the skin between thigh and breast. Using a carving knife as an aid, press the thigh outward to find the hip joint. Hold the drumstick and gently pull it away from the body, at the same time cutting downwards between the leg and the body until you come to the joint that connects the leg to the body. Cut through the joint, not the bone, to separate the two pieces.

Holding the turkey with the carving fork, carve across the breast at the top. If you prefer, you can cut thin slices of meat from the entire length of the breast; first, make a horizontal cut through the breast at the bottom of the bird then, carving parallel to the breastbone, slice diagonally down through the meat until you come to the horizontal cut. Continue until you have carved all the meat on one side. The breast meat should simply fall away in nice, even pieces.

WHAT IS THE CORRECT WAY TO CARVE A CHRISTMAS HAM?

Allow the hot ham to rest, covered, for at least 15 minutes before carving so the juices settle, resulting in a juicier and easier to carve ham. (If you're not heating the ham, remove it from the refrigerator and allow it to come to room temperature for about 1 hour before carving.) Trim two or three slices off the bottom of the ham, parallel to its length, to help stabilise the ham during slicing.

Make a circular cut through the rind about 10cm from the shank end; run your fingers under the edge of the rind then pull rind back from the cut. Reserve the rind to cover the cut surface of the ham to keep it moist during storage.

Hold ham firmly with a carving fork and cut a 1.5cm-deep cut down to the bone next to the rind at the shank end. Placing the knife about 7cm from the cut, slice through the ham on a slight angle to meet the first deep cut; remove wedge of ham. (By removing the wedge the succeeding slices are easier to cut and release from the bone.) Take long sweeps with the knife against the cut surface to carve thin, even slices of ham at an angle.

The meatier part of the ham should be on top and the shank end should always be placed to the carver's right. As you carve, the slices will increase in size; when they get too large, carve the slices from the side to the middle rather than fully across. Alternate sides as you make your slices. Carve slices as thinly as you can; keep the cutting line straight as you carve the ham.

IS THERE ANOTHER WAY TO COOK WHOLE SALMON WITHOUT USING A FISH KETTLE?

A fish kettle makes the cooking of any whole large fish easy. It is a long, narrow stainless steel pan with handles at each end. The fish is placed inside and poached.

If you don't have a fish kettle, the best way to cook a whole salmon is wrapped in several layers of foil and steamed on the barbecue according to the manufacturer's instructions. Top the fish with some herbs, such as bay leaves, thyme or parsley, then add a little liquid and tightly seal in the foil.

If your oven is large enough to take a whole salmon, you can oven-roast the fish in foil.

CONFECTIONERY

Two ways to make caramel

Candy thermometers

Making and using toffee

Rice paper for nougat

Sweetmeat or sweetbread?

WHAT IS THE BEST WAY TO MAKE A CARAMEL FOR A CREME CARAMEL?

Either of the following methods will make a lovely toffee. The sugar-and-water method is easier if you're a beginner.

SUGAR-ONLY METHOD

Spread sugar fairly evenly over the base of a heavy-based frying pan and place over medium to high heat. Do not stir, but turn the pan gently as needed to swirl the sugar for even melting and browning until it is a rich golden-brown colour.

SUGAR-AND-WATER METHOD

Put the amount of sugar and water specified in the recipe into a medium heavy-based saucepan; use a wooden spoon to stir constantly over high heat, without boiling, until the sugar is completely dissolved. If any grains cling to the side of the pan or the spoon, brush them down into the syrup with a wet pastry brush. Once the sugar is dissolved, stop stirring; bring the syrup to the boil and boil rapidly until the mixture is a rich golden-brown colour.

CAN YOU MAKE CARAMEL FROM CANNED CONDENSED MILK?

Yes, this makes a great caramel filling. Pour the can of sweetened condensed milk into a heavy-based saucepan; stir *constantly* for about 10 minutes, over a medium heat, or until the milk is caramelised.

HOW DO YOU USE A CANDY THERMOMETER?

To use a candy thermometer correctly, put it in a small saucepan of cold water and bring it to the boil while you are making the candy mixture (usually a sugar syrup of some sort). When the syrup begins to boil, take the thermometer from the boiling water and put it into the syrup. Leave the thermometer in the syrup until the required temperature is reached. Watch the temperature closely once it reaches 90°C as it can escalate quite quickly. Don't let the thermometer sit in the mixture after it has reached the desired temperature. Return it to the pan of boiling water; remove pan from the heat and cool the thermometer in the water.

Wash, dry and store the thermometer carefully; it's best to store the thermometer wrapped in a tea-towel to protect it from damage.

CAN YOU RECOMMEND THE BEST TYPE OF CANDY THERMOMETER?

Choose a thermometer that is easy to handle when dealing with hot mixtures. It should have a metal body and an adjustable clip or hook so it can be attached to the side of the pan. The most accurate thermometers hold the bulb up and away from the pan's base. Test the thermometer by placing it in a small saucepan of cold water; bring the water to the boil – an accurate thermometer will display 100°C. If the reading is higher or lower, take this difference into account when testing whatever you're cooking. Read the temperature with your eyes at the same level as the measuring liquid in the thermometer; looking from a different angle can result in an inaccurate reading.

I DON'T HAVE A CANDY THERMOMETER. HOW CAN I TEST IF MY TOFFEE IS READY?

First, remove the pan of boiling toffee from the heat, allow the bubbles to subside, then drop a teaspoon of the toffee into a glass of cold tap water; it will set immediately it touches the water. There are different stages of setting, the first is called "small crack", then it goes to "hard crack", and, of course, there are stages in between. The important thing is to make sure the toffee will set enough for your needs.

Lift the toffee out of the water and snap it with your fingers, if you want the toffee darker and harder, return it to the heat and boil it some more. It won't take long – allow for the fact that it will continue to cook, even after it comes off the heat, until the bubbles subside.

HOW DO YOU MAKE TOFFEE?

Toffee is great for decorating cakes, whether it's as fruit or nuts dipped in toffee, shards of toffee speared into the cake surface, or spun toffee over the top. The method is not difficult, but you must exercise great care not to get the boiling toffee on your fingers or hands as it will produce a nasty burn.

Combine the sugar and water as specified in the recipe in a heavy-based saucepan; place over medium to high heat. To prevent crystallisation or graininess, the sugar must be completely dissolved before the mixture boils. Stir constantly until the sugar dissolves; if any sugar grains stick to the sides of the pan, brush them down with a pastry brush that has been dipped in water.

Once the sugar syrup comes to the boil, stop stirring. Boil the syrup, uncovered, about 10 minutes or until the mixture is a golden-brown colour. The longer you cook the toffee the deeper the colour and the harder it will set.

The state described as "hard crack", when the toffee sets pretty much instantly, is achieved between 138°C and 154°C on a candy thermometer. If you don't have one, you can drizzle some of the hot toffee mixture into a container of cold water. If it sets immediately and can be snapped between the fingers, the mixture is at "hard crack"; if not, it should be boiled for a few minutes more. Always remove the pan from the heat and allow the bubbles to subside before testing. Once "hard crack" is achieved, fruit or nuts can be dipped into the toffee. Stand to set on a baking-paper-lined tray.

TOFFEE SHARDS

Use a wooden spoon to drizzle toffee over a baking-paper-lined tray. When the toffee sets, break it and position on the cake.

SPUN TOFFEE

Hold a fork in each hand and dip them in the hot toffee. Bring the backs of the forks together over the cake, draw them apart, dragging the toffee onto the cake. Repeat until you've achieved a "nest" of spun toffee on the top of the cake.

DO I NEED TO USE A CANDY THERMOMETER WHEN MAKING FUDGE AND NOUGAT?

A candy thermometer is a smart investment if you're making confectionery – especially if you're making confectionery like fudge, fondant or nougat where the temperature of the syrup is vital for success.

I AM MAKING NOUGAT AND AM UNSURE OF WHERE TO PURCHASE THE RICE PAPER?

There are two types of rice paper and they are very different. Wafer-thin rectangular rice paper sheets used for confectionery, especially nougat, are made from various plants, not rice. They are usually sold, carefully packaged as they're fragile, in specialty food stores, some health-food stores and kitchenware stores.

Asian rice paper, used mainly for wrapping fresh spring rolls, are rounds or squares of thinly rolled then dried dough made from rice flour; they should not be used in confectionery making.

WHAT IS THE DIFFERENCE BETWEEN SWEETMEATS AND SWEETBREADS?

Sweetmeat is a small piece of something sweet such as a small fancy biscuit, cake or confectionery or candied fruit or nuts. Bonbons, marzipans, pralines and crystallised (candied) fruits are sweetmeats.

Sweetbreads, on the other hand, is the thymus gland (throat) and pancreas (near the stomach) from veal, lamb and pork; it is used in savoury fillings or can be braised, roasted, grilled or poached.

PRESERVING

Sterilising & sealing jam jars

The difference between jam & jelly

How to correctly store preserves

Understanding pectin

Drying chillies & tomatoes

I WOULD LIKE TO MAKE AN ORANGE MARMALADE BUT AM UNSURE OF THE CORRECT WAY TO STERILISE, SEAL AND STORE THE JARS. CAN YOU HELP?

Your storage jars must be glass and without chips or cracks. Just before use, they must be sterilised and dried, using clean hands (use clean tea-towels when holding or moving jars). The hot jam must be added to hot sterilised jars and sealed while still hot.

TO STERILISE JARS

Place the cleaned jars on their sides in a large boiler or saucepan; cover with cold water. Cover the pan and bring to the boil over high heat; boil for 20 minutes. Carefully remove jars from water; drain. Stand, top-side up, on a wooden board. The heat from the jars will cause any remaining water to evaporate quickly. Stand the clean jars, top-side up, on a wooden board placed in a cold oven (do not allow the jars to touch); heat oven temperature to very slow (120°C/100°C fan-forced), then leave the jars in the oven for 30 minutes.

TO SEAL JARS

As soon as the preserves are spooned or poured into the sterilised jars or bottles, they must be correctly sealed to prevent deterioration. Fill jars right to the top, as preserves shrink slightly on cooling.

If sealing with paraffin wax, leave space for the wax to be poured over the preserve. Paraffin wax (available from chemists) is not often used as much these days. Melt wax slowly in a small saucepan over low heat; pour a thin layer over the top of the cooled preserve, about 2mm thick, just enough to cover the surface. Leave until almost set, then pour another thin layer on top of the first layer. Insert small pieces of string in the wax just before it sets to make it easier to remove wax. It is important not to overheat the wax or it will shrink on cooling, giving an imperfect seal.

Metal lids are not suitable unless they have a protective plastic insert or liner; the acid content of the preserve will corrode the lids and the contents will become contaminated. Plastic screw-top lids give a good seal (plastic snap-on lids are not airtight enough). Plastic lids must be well washed, rinsed and dried, or put through the dishwasher.

Some older preserving outfits have glass lids; these can be sterilised in the same way as the jars.

Do not use aluminium foil, cellophane or paper covers for preserves; acid in the preserves will corrode foil, while paper and cellophane are not airtight enough for long-term keeping.

HOW DO I STOP CONDENSATION FORMING UNDER THE LIDS AFTER BOTTLING JAMS AND JELLIES?

To avoid trapped condensation, fill the hot dry jars right to the top, literally as much as the jars will hold. Seal the jars while still hot; this stops the trapped air/condensation syndrome. The jam will contract and shrink slightly away from the lids as they cool down to room temperature. This rule applies to all jams, jellies, pickles and chutneys.

WHAT'S THE BEST PAN TO USE WHEN MAKING JAM?

Use large aluminium, stainless steel or enamel saucepans or boilers; do not use copper or unsealed cast iron pans as the acid in the fruit will damage the metal, and the colour and flavour of the jam or jelly can be affected. The pan needs to be large so evaporation can occur during the boiling process.

MANY PRESERVE RECIPES SAY TO "STORE IN A COOL DARK PLACE". WHAT DOES THIS MEAN?

Most modern homes have heating in every room, so store the preserves in a garage, cellar or under the house where it's cool and the temperature is constant. If the place where you live is wet or humid, then opt for the refrigerator for storage.

WHATS THE DIFFERENCE BETWEEN JAM AND JELLY?

Jam contains fruit pulp or sliced fruit, while jelly is made from the liquid of cooked fruit that has been strained through a fine cloth.

WHAT IS PECTIN?

Pectin is a carbohydrate found in certain fruits which, when combined with acid and sugar, helps a jam, jelly or marmalade to set (jell). Commercial pectin can be bought from health-food stores and some supermarkets; it can be used to set jams and jellies made with fruit low in pectin.

PECTIN LEVELS IN FRUIT

Fruit with a good balance of acid and pectin	Grapes, crab apples, currants, lemons, limes, grapefruit, underripe quinces, sour gooseberries, sour apples, sour guavas, sour oranges, sour plums.
Fruit high in pectin and low in acid	Sweet apples, sweet guavas, sweet quinces. When making jam or jelly from these fruits, add 2 tablespoons lemon juice to each 1kg fruit to increase the acid content.
Fruits low in pectin and high in acid	Apricots, rhubarb, underripe peaches, pineapples. When making jam or jelly from these fruits, add 2 tablespoons lemon juice to each 1kg fruit to increase the pectin content.
Fruits low in acid and pectin (and not suitable alone for making jam or jelly)	Pears, melons, peaches, most varieties of strawberries and cherries. These are usually combined with fruits high in pectin and acid when making jams or jellies.
Berries	Most berries contain only a small amount of pectin, even when slightly underripe, but they can be combined with apples, or can have lemon juice added, to achieve acid/pectin balance.

MY STRAWBERRY JAM JUST WON'T SET, REGARDLESS OF HOW LONG I BOIL IT. WHAT'S WRONG?

Strawberries are one of the fruits that is low in acid and pectin – both of which are required to make jam set; lemon juice can be added and the jam re-boiled until it jells when tested. However, if the jam has darkened in colour and has a caramel taste (which happens when the sugar is overcooked) it cannot be re-boiled.

If the flavour of the jam is still okay, commercial pectin (available in powdered form from health-food stores and supermarkets) can be added to help set the jam; just follow the directions on the packet.

HOW DO I KNOW WHEN MY JAM IS READY?

To test if jam has set (or jelled), remove the pan from the heat and drop a small amount of jam on a chilled plate or saucer. Allow to cool, then gently push a finger through the jam. If the surface wrinkles, the setting point has been reached. If not, return to the boil and retest at 2-minute intervals. You could also use a candy thermometer. Jams (and jellies) will set at 105°C-106°C.

MY JELLY IS ALWAYS CLOUDY, EVEN THOUGH I STRAIN IT. WHAT AM I DOING WRONG?

Leave the fruit mixture to drip through a fine cloth – this can take up to 12 hours. Do not push or force the fruit through the cloth, as this will cause the jelly to become cloudy. Cover the fruit loosely with greaseproof paper or a tea-towel to it protect from dust and insects.

Any scum left on the fruit after it has cooked will also cause the jelly to become cloudy, so skim off any that has appeared on the surface before straining the mixture.

FOR SOME REASON MY JELLY DOESN'T SET. I TRY RE-BOILING IT, LIKE JAM, BUT IT ENDS UP WORSE. WHAT CAN I DO?

A good jelly should be clear and translucent, firm enough to hold its own shape, but soft enough to quiver when cut with a spoon.

Jelly not setting is due to a lack of pectin. If you re-boil the jelly it will lose clarity and texture. While adding commercial pectin will also spoil its appearance, it will, at least, set the jelly; just follow the directions on the packet.

As a last resort, jellies can be set by using a packet of dessert-type jelly crystals. Choose a similar flavour and colour to your homemade jelly, place the jelly crystals in a saucepan with ½ cup water, stir over low heat until dissolved, then add the unset homemade jelly to the mixture; stir over low heat until any lumps are dissolved.

The amount of jelly crystals required will depend on the consistency of your homemade jelly. As a guide, one 100g packet of jelly crystals should set about 3 cups of homemade jelly.

I DON'T HAVE A JELLY BAG. HOW CAN I STRAIN MY JELLY?

The fruit mixture can be strained through a damp clean finely-woven cotton cloth, such as boiled unbleached calico or muslin. At a pinch, a new, finely-woven, damp clean tea-towel will do.

Turn a stool upside down on a table and tie the corners of the cloth securely to the legs of the stool (leave the cloth loose enough to dip in the centre). Place a large bowl under the cloth and pour the fruit and its liquid into the cloth. Cover loosely to protect the mixture from dust and insects, and leave the liquid to drip through the cloth; this will take up to 12 hours.

HOW DO I DRY CHILLIES?

The climate you live in will determine the methods you can use to dry chillies. If you live in a humid climate, you will find that natural air-drying will result in soft, mouldy chillies. If you live in a hot, dry climate, then natural air-drying may be successful.

When drying chillies, choose only mature red fruit, ignoring those with spots or cuts. Using a needle and strong white thread, string chillies through their stems and hang in a sunny spot to dry.

You can also dry them in an electric oven by stretching muslin across a rack, keeping it taut on the sides with skewers or toothpicks, then spreading the chillies, in a single layer, over the muslin. With the oven set very low, say 60°C/40°C fan-forced, prop the door open and dry the chillies until they look brown and crisp. This takes between three and six hours. Drying time will vary depending on the size of the chillies. Cool chillies before storing in airtight containers, or blending or processing them to a powder. A food dehydrator may also be used to dry chillies; follow the manufacturer's directions. Chillies also freeze well.

I HAVE A SMALL BOX OF EGG TOMATOES AND WOULD LIKE TO DRY THEM IN THE OVEN. HOW IS THIS DONE?

Cut the tomatoes in half lengthways and place, cut-side up, on fine wire racks over oven trays. Sprinkle the tomatoes lightly with salt. Dry in the oven at the lowest temperature possible for 6 to 8 hours or until tomatoes are dry to touch; cool. Pack the tomatoes into hot sterilised jars (see page 58) then pour enough olive oil over the tomatoes to cover completely; seal immediately.

For semi-dried tomatoes, follow the above method, but only dry tomatoes for about 3 hours or until they are semi-dried.

Oven-dried and semi-dried tomatoes will keep in the refrigerator for about 1 month.

MEAT & CHICKEN

Cooking meat perfectly on the BBQ

How to stir-fry without stewing

The best cuts for slow cooking

Prosciutto, pancetta & coppa

Cooking a great roast

UNFORTUNATELY NOT ALL MEN ARE WHIZZES AT THE BBQ. MY PARTNER HAS A TENDENCY TO OVERCOOK EVERYTHING SO THAT IT'S DRY ON THE INSIDE OR BLACK ON THE OUTSIDE AND RAW IN THE CENTRE. ARE THERE ANY RULES FOR COOKING MEAT ON THE BBQ?

When cooking chicken on the barbecue, it only needs a moderately-high heat, so don't place it over a direct flame. Cuts on the bone tend to be juicer, so drumsticks, legs and wings are the ideal choices.

Veal has a low fat content so it dries out easily. Cook it over a low heat, away from the flame.

If you want your beef medium-rare, cook it directly over the flame; for well-done, seal the surface over high heat then move to a less hot part of the barbecue to finish off the cooking.

Lamb should be cooked over high heat for medium-rare; for well-done, cook for longer over a medium heat.

Pork needs only a moderate heat; don't overcook pork, it should be slightly pink inside.

Sausages should never be pricked, and must be cooked over a low heat. Poach them first, to reduce the time spent on the barbecue; this helps the inside to cook through while ensuring the outside stays crisp, not burned.

THE MEAT IN MY STIR-FRY IS OFTEN TOUGH AND CHEWY. WHY IS THIS?

It sounds as if you're overcrowding the pan (or wok). When too much meat is added to the pan all at once, it decreases the heat of the pan and stews the meat in its own juices, causing it to become tough and chewy. The pan should be at a high temperature and the meat should be seared in small batches to seal in the juices. If stir-frying marinated meat, thoroughly drain the marinade before cooking. Cut the meat into thin strips across the grain, this shortens the fibre, making the pieces more tender.

WHAT ARE THE BEST CUTS OF MEAT TO USE WHEN SLOW COOKING?

Slow cooking is not only flavoursome, it's budget-friendly; tougher (and therefore cheaper) cuts of meat are ideal for slow cooking, becoming juicy and tender over the long cooking time. And, while the actual cooking time is long, preparation tends to be short – after putting all the ingredients into the pan, you can leave it to simmer while you get on with other things. Some of the best cuts are:

Beef: topside, oyster, blade, skirt, round and chuck steaks, gravy beef.

Veal: osso buco, shanks, shoulder.

Lamb: neck chops, boneless shoulder, shanks, boneless forequarter.

Pork: forequarter chops, neck, diced shoulder, pork belly.

Chicken: any pieces, but those on the bone work best (drumstick, thighs, marylands).

WHEN MAKING A CASSEROLE, WHY DO I HAVE TO BROWN THE MEAT BEFORE PUTTING IT INTO THE OVEN?

The first stage of the cooking process often involves coating the meat with flour and browning it in butter and/or oil. This gives the meat a coating that seals in the flavour and juices. The flour also thickens the liquid during cooking, while browning imparts a good rich colour to the casserole.

Toss the meat in the flour just before browning. Don't do this ahead of time as the meat juices will absorb the flour and the coating will become gluey. Sear the meat quickly, in batches, over a medium-high heat until the pieces are golden brown and sealed on all sides. Do not crowd the pan as this will stew the meat, rather than browning it.

HOW DO I KNOW WHEN MY ROAST BEEF IS COOKED?

Insert a meat thermometer into the centre of the thickest part, away from any bone – the roast is cooked when the temperature is 63°C for medium-rare, 71°C for medium and 77°C for well-done.

If you don't have a meat thermometer, insert a fine skewer into the centre of the meat towards the end of the cooking time, and check the juice that runs out – red juice means rare, pink means medium, clear means well-done. To enhance juiciness, rest the meat, wrapped in foil, for 15 minutes before serving.

You may find the cooking times, below, useful next time you are making roast beef.
Rare: 240°C/220°C fan-forced for 15 minutes then 180°C/160°C fan-forced for 15 minutes per 500g.
Medium: 220°C/200°C fan-forced for 15 minutes then 180°C/160°C fan-forced for 20 minutes per 500g.
Well-done: 220°C/200°C fan-forced for 10 minutes then 180°C/160°C fan-forced for 25 minutes per 500g.

IS IT TRUE THAT CUTTING MEAT AGAINST THE GRAIN WILL GIVE A MORE TENDER CUT?

Yes, meat should always be cut against the grain for maximum tenderness (unless a recipe states otherwise). Meat is composed of small and large muscle fibres. The "grain" of the meat is the direction in which these fibres run. Cutting against the grain severs these fibres, making the meat more tender.

HOW CAN I TELL WHEN MY STEAKS ARE COOKED MEDIUM-RARE?

Press the surface of the steak with a finger or use the back of a pair of tongs. Rare steak feels soft and spongy; medium-rare feels soft and springy; medium-done feels firm but still springy; and well-done feels quite firm. Rest the steaks, wrapped or covered with foil, for 5 minutes before serving.

IS THERE ANY DIFFERENCE BETWEEN PANCETTA, PROSCIUTTO AND COPPA?

Pancetta is a kind of unsmoked bacon: pork belly is cured in salt and spices then rolled into a sausage shape and dried for several weeks. It is usually used sliced or chopped as an ingredient, or to add flavour, rather than eaten on its own.

Prosciutto, by comparison, is more like ham: it is traditionally salted, air-cured and aged, then eaten raw.

Coppa is pork shoulder or neck that has been lightly seasoned with garlic and herbs and marinated in red wine. It is then salted and hung to dry for at least six months to cure.

WHAT IS THE DIFFERENCE BETWEEN SPARE RIBS AND SHORT RIBS, AND HOW DO YOU COOK THEM?

Pork spare ribs are sold in long slabs or racks of 10 to 12 ribs, trimmed so that little fat remains. They are a long cut from the lower portion of the pig, specifically the belly and breastbone. These are often called American-style ribs and are the best ones to slather with homemade barbecue sauce and cook on the barbie.

Short ribs, on the other hand, are usually beef. They can be "on the bone" or "boneless." The meat is flavourful but very tough. Short ribs are usually braised slowly in liquid before being cooked, but can be grilled successfully at low temperatures if they have been marinated first.

I WAS SERVED PINK PORK AT A RESTAURANT – IS IT SAFE TO EAT?

Pork is at its juiciest when cooked with a hint of pink in the middle. It dries out when overcooked. Pork should be cooked at a moderate, not high, heat for best results.

WHAT IS BUTTERFLIED LAMB?

Butterflied lamb is lamb that has been cut down the centre, cutting almost, but not completely, through. The two halves are then opened flat to resemble a butterfly. Thick cuts, like loin chops, are often butterflied so that they cook more quickly. Butterflied leg of lamb is a completely boned leg, trimmed of excess fat and spread flat for cooking.

WHAT TYPE OF CUT IS A NOISETTE?

Noisettes are small round steaks cut from a rolled and tied boneless rack of lamb. They're very tender and can be cooked quickly.

I WAS TOLD THAT I SHOULD PUT A LEG OF LAMB ON A WIRE RACK TO ROAST – NOT JUST STRAIGHT INTO THE PAN. WHY? MY GRANDMOTHER NEVER USED A WIRE RACK FOR ROASTING IN HER LIFE, AND HER ROASTS WERE ALWAYS PERFECT.

There is really no one right way here. Some people put their meat straight into the pan, some use a rack and some use oven bags. Putting a roast on a rack means the bottom of the meat does not stew in any juices and go soggy. One benefit of using a rack is that the oven heat circulates more evenly around the meat, creating more even cooking. Also, a rack means the meat isn't resting on the bottom of the hot pan so there is less chance that it will overcook.

HOW LONG SHOULD I COOK LAMB SO THAT IT IS MEDIUM DONE?

Lamb legs and shoulders should be roasted at 180°C/160°C fan-forced for 20-25 minutes per 500g for rare; 25-30 minutes per 500g for medium and 30-35 minutes per 500g for well-done.

MY CHICKEN ROAST ALWAYS DRIES OUT. HOW DO I KEEP IT MOIST?

This can happen when the oven temperature is too high or the chicken is cooked for too long. Try covering the chicken with greased foil for an hour, then remove the foil to brown the chicken in the remaining cooking time.

Another trick is to roast the chicken breast-side down. Or, to prevent the breast drying out, cover it with criss-crossed bacon rashers. In this case, don't cook the chicken under foil.

To test if a chicken is cooked, insert a small metal skewer into the thickest part of the thigh. If the juices run clear, it is cooked; if they're pink the chicken needs more cooking. If there aren't any juices, then the chicken is overcooked.

MY COOKED CHICKEN BREASTS ARE ALWAYS DRY. HOW DO I COOK THEM SO THEY STAY MOIST?

Toughness and dryness is usually caused by overcooking, which happens if the temperature of the pan or oven is too hot – the outside cooks quickly to a thick, crust-like edge, while the inside takes longer to cook. Cooking chicken breast at a lower temperature can help avoid this problem.

Chicken breasts are quite thick, but they also have a thin part, so you need to cook the breast for a long time to ensure the middle is cooked. By then, the thin part of the breast is overcooked and tough. Avoid this problem by cutting the breast lengthways, or hitting it with a meat mallet so it is of a more even thickness throughout and is thinner, so it can be cooked for less overall time.

Testing the breast for doneness by cutting into it releases any juices trapped in the flesh that would keep it moist. Check small pieces by pressing with a pair of tongs, or your finger; they should feel springy.

Finally, chicken breast is naturally tough because it doesn't have very much fat and is also not on the bone – poultry cuts on the bone will always be more tender and juicer than those without.

SEAFOOD

Preparing shellfish

Cleaning and filleting fish

How to humanely kill a lobster

Selecting fish for sashimi

The best way to pan-fry fish

WHAT DOES IT MEAN TO "BEARD" MUSSELS AND HOW IT IS DONE?

It does seem a curious choice of word because it doesn't mean that a mussel is aged. The "beard" is the common name for the byssal threads – the fibres that hold the mussels firmly to rocks and other mussels in the seabed. Scrub the mussels all over with a stiff brush before bearding them.

To remove the beard, hold a single mussel with your fingers (sometimes using a small towel helps provide a better grip) and give an abrupt tug down and away from the hinge; if the beard is pulled out the opposite way, the mussel inside the shell can be torn and even killed. Discard the byssal threads and rinse the mussels again under cold water; dry with absorbent paper before cooking them.

WHAT IS THE CORRECT WAY TO DEVEIN AN UNSHELLED, UNCOOKED PRAWN?

There is no one "right" way to devein a prawn. Small prawns don't have to be deveined except for aesthetic reasons, but king prawns – with their larger intestinal vein – can feel unpleasant in the mouth. A simple way to remove this vein is to shell the prawn then slit down the back, revealing the intestinal vein. Hold the prawn, cut-side up, in one hand then, with the other hand, insert a toothpick under the vein in the centre of the back. Lift carefully, but firmly, and the vein will come out.

DO YOU NEED TO DO ANYTHING TO PIPIS, CLAMS AND COCKLES BEFORE COOKING THEM?

Wash in several changes of water; scrub shells with a stiff brush and cleanse by soaking in salted water (100g sea salt per 4 litres) for several hours.

HOW DO I OPEN OYSTERS?

Protect your non-opening hand with either a tough glove, or a tea-towel wrapped around the oyster; lever an oyster knife (also known as an oyster shucker), or another short, pointed, rigid-bladed knife, between the shells at the hinge, and twist to pop the shells apart.

Cut through the muscle joining the oyster to the shell; discard the top shell (try to save any oyster liquor for added natural flavour). Place the bottom half of the shell, with the oyster, on a tray with a bed of rock salt to hold the oysters upright.

HOW DO I OPEN LIVE SCALLOPS BEFORE COOKING THEM?

Scallops bought on or off the shell are usually prepared already – simply remove any small brown parts that are left. If the recipe specifies white meat only, gently detach the orange roe with your fingers and, if you wish, keep it for another dish.

To open live scallops, put them on ice. When they start to open, hold each one, dark-side up and hinge facing away, insert the point of a strong knife from the right-hand side between shells and slide along to cut the hinge. Discard the top shell and peel the dark mantle and gut off the pale meat by scraping from hinge to front, pinching the mantle firmly to the knife. Slide the knife under the meat to separate it from the shell and trim off any remaining dark threads or wispy brown beard.

HOW DO I TENDERISE OCTOPUS?

To tenderise octopus, first pound it with a heavy mallet, then rub with salt; rub the skin off under running water. Baby octopus should not need tenderising, but if in doubt, freeze them overnight then thaw, which partially breaks down the structure of the flesh and makes them more tender.

HOW DO I PREPARE WHOLE BABY OCTOPUS?

Cut off the head/body section below the eyes to remove the tentacles in one piece. Push the beak up through the centre of the tentacles, cut off and discard. If using the body, cut out the eyes with kitchen shears or a very sharp knife then turn the body inside out and discard all organs and the ink sac, unless it is to be used in the recipe. Rinse well.

I WOULD LIKE TO TRY COOKING CALAMARI. HOW DO I PREPARE IT?

Calamari, squid and cuttlefish are known as cephalopods, or molluscs without shells, with the calamari being a tender, eminently edible, variety of squid. Pull the head and tentacles from the body; the intestines will come out with them. Cut off the tentacles in one piece, then press the centre and discard the beak that pops out, along with the head and intestines. Remove the transparent quill from inside the body, and pull off the fins. Dip your fingers in salt and rub off the skin from the body, fins and tentacles. Rinse well.

WHAT IS THE MOST HUMANE WAY TO KILL A LIVE LOBSTER?

The most acceptable method of killing lobster and other crustaceans (as demanded by RSPCA Australia) is to chill them to render them insensible. Crustaceans are cold blooded animals; when their temperature is reduced their activity slows and eventually they become numbed. Once chilled, crustaceans must be killed by spiking the nerve centre. Live crustaceans should never be put into boiling water without first being chilled to render them insensible. Freeze live lobsters, bugs and scampi for at least 2 hours before cooking. Kill yabbies and marron by freezing for 2 hours.

WHAT IS THE BEST WAY TO PREPARE COOKED LOBSTER?

Place lobster upside-down on a chopping board; hold the tail where it joins the body to flatten it out. Carefully plunge a large, heavy and very sharp knife through the lobster to the chopping board then cut in half lengthways through the centre of the body and tail. Turn the lobster around and cut in half down through the centre of the head. Chop the claws and legs off the body; crack the claws with the back of the knife and extract the meat from the claws and legs. Pull the two halves apart and, using a small spoon, scoop out and discard the liver and brain matter. Rinse under cold water then press the shell on both sides to loosen the meat; it should come out in a single large piece.

HOW DO I PREPARE COOKED CRAB?

Twist off the legs and claws, lift tail flap then, with a peeling motion, lift off the back shell. Discard the whitish gills, liver and brain matter.

Rinse the crab, then crack the body shell and pick out the meat, breaking the shell as needed. Crack the claws with nutcrackers; break the legs in half and extract meat from these, using a skewer to help if necessary.

HOW DO YOU BONE FISH?

Cut off the head of the fish behind the gills. Slit the belly and remove the entrails. Open the belly out and "stand" the fish upright. Press along the back to loosen the backbone, then ease it off the flesh. Cut off at the tail.

WHAT IS PIN-BONING?

This is removing all the tiny, hidden bones from a fish fillet. Run your fingers firmly along the fillet, then, starting from the tail end, use tweezers to pull out each bone as you feel it.

MY NOW-RETIRED HUSBAND HAS TAKEN UP FISHING. HOW DO WE GUT AND CLEAN HIS CATCH?

This is a messy business and is best done outside. To scale the catch, spread plenty of newspaper around as the scales will fly. Grasp the tail with salted fingers (this makes gripping the tail easier) and use a serrated fish-scaler or rigid knife to scrape firmly from tail to head. Repeat on the other side.

Next, slit the fish open along the belly from the vent (near the tail) to the head, pull out all intestinal matter and scrape away any dark blood from the backbone. Rinse well.

To fillet the fish, remove the head. Dip the fingers of one hand into salt then, holding and starting from the tail, use a thin, flexible knife to cut along the backbone towards the head. Remove the meat in one piece. Repeat on the other side. For flat fish, cut down the centre and remove the fillets on each side.

To skin the fillets, place them on a board, skin-side down and tail end towards you. Dip fingers of one hand in salt and hold the tail end firmly. Use the other hand to ease a thin knife between the flesh and skin, pushing rather than cutting the flesh off the skin.

WHAT ARE WHITE FISH FILLETS?

You could use blue eye, snapper, barramundi, swordfish, bream, flake, gemfish, john dory, kingfish, ling, jewfish, mahi mahi, red emperor, whiting, cod, haddock and flathead.

HOW DO I PREPARE SASHIMI?

Specify sashimi-grade tuna (or kingfish, bream, mackerel or jewfish) when buying the fish, and only buy from a reputable fish market. Wrap the fish tightly in plastic wrap and freeze until just firm. Immediately on removing from the freezer and unwrapping, use a heavy, sharp knife to slice the fish as thinly as possible. Serve immediately.

WHAT IS CEVICHE?

Ceviche, pronounced *se-vee-chay*, is a Latin-American specialty. It is a type of citrus-marinated seafood salad. Thinly sliced raw fish is marinated in lime juice, which essentially cooks it without exposing it to heat. The fish is marinated until the flesh is firm and opaque.

HOW DO I KNOW THAT THE SEAFOOD I'M BUYING IS FRESH?

Fresh seafood (fish and shellfish) should always be bought from seafood markets or a reputable fishmonger. All seafood should look fresh and have a fresh "sea" smell – any seafood that smells "fishy" is no good to eat.

Whole fish should have firm, not spongy, flesh with red gills; the skin should be shiny with close fitting scales and the eyes should be clear and bright.

Fish fillets and cutlets should have moist flesh with a firm texture; there should be no signs of discolouration or dryness. Any bones should be firmly attached to the flesh.

Crustaceans and molluscs should have brightly coloured shells or flesh, and the tentacles, heads, flesh or shells should be plump, firm and intact. Shells should be closed, or should close when tapped on a bench. There should also be no discolouration of the joints.

WHY DO YOU FLOUR FISH BEFORE PAN-FRYING?

Flouring fish should be done just before the frying process. Coat the fish lightly in flour, then pan-fry in a little butter, oil (vegetable, olive or peanut are best) or a combination of both (use just enough to cover the base of the pan). The flour protects the delicate flesh of the fish and gives it a delicious crisp coating.

PULSES & GRAINS

How to cook the perfect rice

The secret behind creamy risotto

What are blue boilers & cowpeas?

A quick way to cook dried beans

Is it polenta or cornmeal?

HOW DO YOU COOK PERFECT LONG-GRAIN RICE?

There are several methods for cooking rice, and the best is probably in an electric rice cooker. But if you don't have one, the stove top absorption method produces the best results.

Start by thoroughly rinsing the rice under cold running water until the water runs clear – at least two to three times. (Basmati rice can be soaked for 30 minutes rather than rinsed.) This washes away the fine coating of powdery starch that is produced by the grains rubbing against each other.

For long-grain rice, bring 1 cup of rice and 1½ cups of water to the boil, stirring occasionally. Lower the heat to medium/low level, cover the saucepan with a tight-fitting lid, and simmer for 12-15 minutes. Remove from the heat, and stand with the lid still on for 5-10 minutes. For firmer rice add a little less water; for softer rice, add slightly more water. If cooking large quantities of rice, the amount of water to rice ratio will be reduced.

Rice is ideally cooked to "al dente", that is, soft but with a slightly firm centre). Pinch a grain between your fingers to test it. To finish, fluff rice with a fork, or use a spatula to slice through the rice rather than stir it so that you don't mash the rice.

WHY IS IT IMPORTANT TO USE HOT STOCK WHEN MAKING RISOTTO?

The creamy texture so characteristic of risotto can only be achieved by the use of a starchy short-grained rice, such as arborio, and hot stock. The hot stock acts as a kind of melding agent, releasing the starch grains into the stock and making the mixture creamy. The rice should not be rinsed before being used.

THERE ARE SO MANY WAYS TO COOK RICE. WHICH IS THE BEST?

The aim is to cook the rice until the grains are tender, but still separate, rather than stuck together in lumps. There are four main methods of achieving this (see below); you can choose whichever method suits you best. The microwave cooking times, below, are for an 830 watt microwave oven.

WHITE RICE

METHOD	QUANTITY OF RICE	QUANTITY OF WATER	COOKING TIME
Absorption	1½ cups (300g)	3 cups (750ml)	10 minutes
Microwave	1½ cups (300g)	3 cups (750ml)	10 minutes
Baked	1½ cups (300g)	2½ cups (625ml)	25 minutes
Boiled	1½ cups (300g)	8 cups (2 litres)	12 minutes

BROWN RICE

METHOD	QUANTITY OF RICE	QUANTITY OF WATER	COOKING TIME
Absorption	1½ cups (300g)	3½ cups (875ml)	30 minutes
Microwave	1½ cups (300g)	3½ cups (875ml)	25 minutes
Baked	1½ cups (300g)	3½ cups (875ml)	1 hour
Boiled	1½ cups (300g)	8 cups (2 litres)	25 minutes

WILD RICE

METHOD	QUANTITY OF RICE	QUANTITY OF WATER	COOKING TIME
Absorption	½ cup (100g)	1½ cups (375ml)	40 minutes
Microwave	½ cup (100g)	2 cups (500ml)	25 minutes
Baked	½ cup (100g)	½ cup (125ml)	30 minutes
Boiled	½ cup (100g)	4 cups (1 litre)	20 minutes

I'M TOLD FRENCH DU PUY LENTILS ARE NO LONGER IMPORTED INTO AUSTRALIA. WHY?

Quarantine restrictions on imports of the French-grown du puy lentils determined that the legume had to undergo specific processing before being brought into Australia. Unfortunately, this process caused the lentil to be all but useless for the manner of cooking for which it is best suited.

Named after the French town of Le Puy-en-Velay, in the Auvergne, these tiny, blue-green-skinned lentils possess a delicate flavour and a texture that holds up through boiling – it doesn't become mush, like other lentils.

All is not lost, though, as Australian-grown substitutes are available, variously sold as french green lentils, bondi lentils or matilda lentils. While our versions aren't exactly the same, due to the different climate, they have a lovely nutty flavour and stand up well to being boiled.

HOW DO YOU COOK PASTA AL DENTE?

Al dente (al *den* tay) is Italian meaning "to the tooth", and describes a food that is cooked only until it offers a slight resistance when bitten into – it should not be soft or overdone.

Bring water to a rolling boil in a large saucepan then add salt (salt increases the water temperature slightly at boiling point). Gradually add the pasta so the water does not go off the boil. Add long pasta by holding the strands and feeding them in gradually as they soften. Keep the water boiling fast to keep the pasta moving.

Test by biting a piece of pasta. It is done when it is al dente – cooked through but still firm to the bite (2 to 3 minutes for fresh pasta, 5 to 12 minutes, depending on freshness and thickness, for dried).

Drain pasta, but do not rinse. Place pasta into a heated serving bowl, add the sauce then toss and serve at once. Serve the cheese separately, if using.

I'VE GOT A RECIPE THAT CALLS FOR SOMETHING KNOWN AS "BLUE BOILERS". WHAT ARE THESE?

Blue boilers, also known as dried peas, cowpeas or field peas, are the classic (mushy) pea for a pie floater. They are hard, round, bluish-green peas grown specifically for drying. They are available packaged in supermarkets and health-food stores.

IS THERE A QUICK WAY TO SOAK DRIED BEANS? SOMETIMES I FORGET TO SOAK THEM BEFORE I NEED THEM.

Place the dried beans in a large saucepan and generously cover them with cold water. Bring to the boil, then cover and cook for 2 minutes. Remove from the heat and stand for 1 hour then drain.

If you wish, when soaking dried beans overnight, soak double or triple the amount of beans required then freeze the remainder (well-drained), in individual cup measures, for later use. This way, you'll always have beans ready to cook, even if you forget to soak them overnight.

WHAT'S THE DIFFERENCE BETWEEN POLENTA AND CORNMEAL?

Polenta is also known as cornmeal. It is a flour-like cereal made of dried corn (maize) and is ground into varying degrees of fineness/coarseness.

Polenta is also the name of the dish made from it, and can be either served soft and creamy (with just the addition of a liquid) or can be spread into a shallow pan and chilled until firm before being grilled, pan-fried or barbecued.

DAIRY & EGGS

Half & half – what is it?

The lowdown on creams & butters

Cheese & its uses

Egg whites – storing & whipping

Poach the perfect egg

SOME RECIPES IN AMERICAN COOKBOOKS ASK FOR 'HALF AND HALF' – WHAT IS THIS?

Half and half, or half and half milk, is a term used in North American recipes; it is a mixture of half milk and half cream. It has 10-12% milk fat and cannot be whipped.

WHAT IS THE AUSTRALIAN EQUIVALENT OF DOUBLE CREAM AND SINGLE CREAM?

In Australia, the labels "single" and "double" cream are mostly irrelevant. You need to read the fat content on the label to see which is which.

Single cream (often labelled "pouring cream") contains 33-35% fat, double cream has 60-66% fat, and thickened cream is single cream with a thickening agent added.

HOW DO I MAKE HOMEMADE SOUR CREAM?

You can make 1 cup of cream sour by adding 1 or 2 teaspoons lemon juice or white vinegar to regular pouring cream, but it will not produce the same thick results as packaged sour cream.

HOW CAN I MAKE MY OWN CRÈME FRAÎCHE?

This thick, tangy cream can be made by combining 1½ cups thick (double) cream with ¾ cup sour cream in a medium bowl. Cover and stand at cool room temperature for 5-6 hours. Store, covered, in the refrigerator for up to 1 week.

WHAT IS ONE AMERICAN STICK OF BUTTER EQUAL TO IN AUSTRALIA?

1 stick (4oz) butter is equivalent to 125g.

WHY DO RECIPES OFTEN CALL FOR UNSALTED BUTTER? WOULD USING ORDINARY BUTTER MAKE ANY DIFFERENCE TO THE RESULT? HOW WOULD USING CLARIFIED BUTTER, UNSALTED BUTTER, MARGARINE, ETC., AFFECT A RECIPE?

Unsalted butter, often called "sweet" butter, simply has no added salt. The salt content of regular salted butter is sometimes discernable in a sweet recipe, especially with chocolate. You can use regular butter in most cakes and baking, but it's advisable to stick to unsalted butter when it's specified in delicate toppings, icings and so on.

Cultured unsalted butter is unsalted butter with a culture added to give it a distinctive, slightly sour taste, similar to sour cream and yogurt. Many chefs prefer it for its slightly lighter result.

Clarified butter, or ghee, is almost pure milk fat and is mostly used in cooking and for frying, as it can reach higher temperatures than regular butter before burning.

Cooking margarine is suitable to substitute for butter in most cases for baking, as it has a similar consistency. However, in a recipe that relies on the flavour of butter, such as butter cake and shortbread, it's preferable to use regular butter.

Margarine spreads are often not suitable for baking, as they're too soft and unstable to cream with sugar, which helps to aerate cake mixtures.

I'VE HEARD YOU CAN MAKE YOUR OWN CLARIFIED BUTTER. HOW IS THIS DONE?

To make your own clarified butter, simply melt some butter in a pan over low heat, then allow it to stand until the milk solids settle on the bottom. Gently skim off the clear liquid on top – this is the clarified butter.

WHEN AN AMERICAN RECIPE ASKS FOR "SHORTENING" WHAT CAN I SUBSTITUTE?

Shortening is a generic term for a solid fat, and the American shortening used for most baking is a type of cooking margarine. Either butter or cooking margarine can be used, and one can be substituted for the other.

IS THERE A TRICK TO FRYING OR GRILLING HALOUMI? EITHER IT ENDS UP COLLAPSING BEFORE IT BROWNS, OR IT BECOMES TOUGH.

Haloumi is native to Cyprus where it's a traditional village cheese made of sheep milk and matured in brine. While this makes it sound like fetta, haloumi really resembles mozzarella in texture and cooking properties. It is firm, yet pliable like mozzarella, doesn't melt when warmed, is chewy rather than crumbly when bitten into, and has a salty, subtle sweet flavour.

A stretched-curd cheese, haloumi is great for cooking: it is one of the few cheeses to hold its shape under heat, it can be baked, pan-fried or grilled until golden brown and slightly crisp. If you're having problems cooking haloumi, it's probably because your pan isn't hot enough when the cheese hits the surface, so it ends up stewing on the inside rather than searing on the outside.

Hot and quick is the way to go when frying or grilling haloumi, and eating it as soon as it comes off the heat is essential because it toughens upon cooling. Cooking haloumi on the barbecue gives it a fabulous flavour; it is also great drizzled with a little extra virgin olive oil and a squeeze of lemon juice.

I HAVE SEEN CHEFS ON TV USING MASCARPONE. WHAT IS IT?

People are often confused about whether to regard mascarpone as a cheese or a thick cream. It is, in fact, a fresh triple-cream cheese originating in Italy's Lombardy region, and probably first became known to us when tiramisu was the dessert du jour in the mid-1980s.

Made from cultured cows' milk, its texture can be compared to that of softened butter. It can be spread over a cake to ice it, or as a dip for pieces of firm fresh fruit. Many Italians stir a substantial dollop into risotto just before serving and a great many pasta dishes call for it.

Like most wonderful things, there is no real substitute for mascarpone, but some recipes can be adapted to use soft cream cheese, sour cream or ricotta – or blends of all three.

WHAT'S THE DIFFERENCE BETWEEN PARMIGIANO-REGGIANO AND GRANA PADANO CHEESE?

The generic name for both cheeses is parmesan – the hard, grainy cows'-milk cheese from the northern Italian regions of Reggio Emilia and Parma.

Parmigiano-Reggiano has a crystal-like flake – a result of its minimum 24-month ageing process – and can be identified by its name, stencilled into the pale wax rind in red dots. Its scent is both fragrant and savoury, its taste nutty and delicately pungent and often sharp, tingly and creamy at the same time. Parmigiano-Reggiano is fabulous on a cheese platter with fruit or flaked onto a risotto.

Grana Padano is lower in fat, often less aged, less expensive and with less of a "kick" on the palate. Usually it is finely grated and sprinkled over simple pasta sauces or a salad.

WHAT IS PIZZA CHEESE? IS IT A TYPE OF PARMESAN CHEESE?

Pizza cheese is a commercial blend of varying proportions of processed grated mozzarella, cheddar and parmesan cheeses. It is readily available in major supermarkets.

WHILE WHIPPING EGG WHITES, I HAD A PROBLEM GETTING THEM TO HOLD THEIR SHAPE. WAS THERE SOME PROBLEM WITH THE EGGS OR DOES IT HAVE SOMETHING TO DO WITH THE WEATHER?

All your equipment must be perfectly dry and completely grease-free and clean. Just a trace of oil or fat can stop eggs from forming peaks. Ensure all your utensils are clean by washing them in hot, soapy water with clean wash cloths, and rinsing with boiling water. Dry carefully with a fresh tea-towel. Make sure there's no grease in your bowl or mixer, by wiping them with a piece of absorbent paper that has been dipped in lemon juice or vinegar. Also wash your hands in hot, soapy water and dry them with a clean towel.

The whites must have absolutely no trace of yolk – even the tiniest amount can stop peaks from forming. To separate eggs, have two dry, grease-free bowls and a cup at hand. Separate one egg into the cup. Drop the yolk into one bowl and pour the white from the cup into the other bowl. Separate eggs one at a time, so that if you accidentally break one yolk, you haven't ruined the whole batch.

Egg whites are beaten to either soft or firm peak stage. Soft peaks mean the whites barely support themselves and the peak will usually lean over and curl to one side. Firm peak is the stage where the egg white is glossy and smooth and will hold its shape.

HOW CAN I TELL IF MY EGGS ARE FRESH? ARE THEY OK TO USE IF THE SHELLS HAVE SMALL CRACKS?

Place an unbroken raw egg in a tall glass of water. If it's fresh it will sink, if not, it will float. Refrigerating eggs in their cardboard cartons will help keep them fresh. You should check and discard any eggs that have cracks in their shells, as they can contain bacteria that may be harmful.

HOW DO I SHELL HARD-BOILED EGGS WITHOUT TAKING PIECES OF THE WHITE LAYER OFF?

Run cold water over the boiled eggs for about a minute until they're cool enough to handle. Gently smash them, one at a time, against the side of the sink until they're finely cracked all over. Return the eggs to the pan and submerge in cold water for about 5 minutes; drain then pull away the shells and membrane – they should come off easily.

MY POACHED EGGS ARE ALWAYS WATERY OR TOUGH. HOW DO I POACH THE PERFECT EGG?

There are several ways to poach eggs; this method is good for beginners. Put a frying pan of water on to boil. There should be enough water in the pan to completely cover the eggs, about 5cm or so. The eggs need to be fresh and straight from the fridge as cold eggs hold their shape better. Reduce the water to a simmer before adding the eggs (boiling water will toughen them). Break an egg into a small cup then slide it gently into the pan. As the eggs are poaching, spoon a little of the water gently over the tops. The eggs will take about three or four minutes to poach.

Gently lift the eggs from the water with a slotted spoon and drain on paper towel. The white should be set but not hard or rubbery, while the yolk should be soft.

SHOULD EGGS BE STORED IN THE REFRIGERATOR?

Eggs should be stored in the refrigerator in their carton to reduce water loss through the shell. The storage life for eggs is determined by the storage temperatures during distribution. Most stores do not keep eggs under refrigeration and, depending how long the eggs have been stored at room temperature, the potential shelf life will be affected.

HEALTH

Allergies – nut, dairy & egg

Substitutes for gluten

Fixing undercooked brown rice

Getting 8 glasses a day

How to get your daily 2 & 5

I HAVE FOUND MANY RECIPES CALLING FOR NUT MEAL, BUT I HAVE AN ALLERGY TO ALL NUTS. WHAT CAN I USE INSTEAD?

Regrettably, there is no substitute for nut meal that gives the same texture to cakes. You could try substituting desiccated coconut in recipes where nut meal is used only in small quantities.

MY HUSBAND IS UNABLE TO HAVE GLUTEN. CAN I SIMPLY SUBSTITUTE GLUTEN-FREE FLOUR FOR WHEAT FLOUR WITH SUCCESS?

In many instances you can adapt recipes containing gluten flour. When substituting gluten-free flour for wheat flour, you usually get the best results with recipes that have a small quantity of flour in them.

Gluten is a sticky substance that stops baked goods from crumbling and improves their texture by trapping pockets of air. You can replicate the effects of gluten by adding xanthum/xanthan gum, pre-gel starch or guar gum in the approximate proportions of 1 teaspoon to 1 cup of flour. You can buy these gums from some health-food shops and The Coeliac Society. In some recipes it is possible to avoid flour altogether by using ground nuts (nut meal) instead.

MY SON IS BOTH SOYA AND LACTOSE INTOLERANT. WHAT CAN I USE AS A SUBSTITUTE FOR MILK WHEN BAKING?

Rice milk and almond milk are options for you to experiment with. You could try substituting both rice milk and almond milk in recipes where regular milk is used in small quantities. Unfortunately, when used in larger quantities the outcome will depend on the other ingredients in the recipe and how they react together.

CAN I ALTER MY RECIPES TO SUIT MY CHILD'S DAIRY INTOLERANCE?

Having a dairy intolerance means having to avoid all products labelled as containing milk, lactose, butter, margarine, cheese, cream, yogurt, whey, milk solids, non-fat milk products, skimmed milk powder, lactoglobulin, casein, lactalbumin or sodium caseinate. This usually applies to sheep, goat, buffalo and horse milk products as well as those made from cows' milk.

Fortunately, you can use soy milk and any soy milk products as a substitute. Sometimes fat from butter can be replaced with olive or other vegetable oils and on other occasions, fruit juice can make up the liquid component supplied by the milk.

I TRY TO EAT A SENSIBLE DIET, BUT MY BROWN RICE ALWAYS SEEMS UNDERCOOKED AND TOO DRY. AM I COOKING IT WRONGLY?

All rices respond differently to cooking. Brown rice, which has not had its bran layer removed after hulling, takes a little longer to cook. Boil it in a large pan of water until just tooth-tender. If you like it softer, boil it for a minute or two more, then drain.

You can also use the absorption method; this uses twice as much water as rice (½ cup of raw rice per serving). After it boils, simmer, covered tightly, for about 30 minutes, then remove from the heat. Stand, covered, for about 10 minutes to let it steam until tender. Never rinse brown rice after cooking.

IS THERE A GELATINE PRODUCT THAT IS OKAY FOR VEGETARIANS?

There are a number of vegetarian setting agents on the market, agar is among them, however, you could also consider arrowroot, guar gum and xanthan gum. You can find these products in some supermarkets and health-food stores. Follow the directions on the package for optimum results.

I HAVE AN EGG ALLERGY. IS IT POSSIBLE TO LEAVE EGGS OUT OF A RECIPE OR CAN THEY BE SUBSTITUTED?

You should avoid any products that are labelled as containing albumin, dried egg, egg white, yolk, protein or solids, globulin, livetin, lysozyme, ovalbumin, ovoglobulin, ovomucin, ovomucid, ovovitellin or vitellin and pasteurised, powdered or whole egg.

Sometimes you can leave out the eggs in a recipe that calls for only one or two and replace them by adding water. However this is not recommended with most baking recipes, so you will need to either use commercial egg substitutes (available from most supermarkets) or experiment with other substitutions. If the purpose of the egg is to bind the ingredients, you can try substituting mashed banana, apple puree, soft tofu or gelatine dissolved in hot water. If the egg is required as a thickening or setting agent you could use wheat, rice or cornflour blended to a paste with a little water to do the job.

CAN YOU COUNT FRESH FRUIT JUICE AS PART OF YOUR DAILY FRUIT INTAKE, EVEN THOUGH IT DOESN'T CONTAIN FIBRE?

Yes, a fresh fruit juice can be counted as part of your daily 2 fruit servings (and as part of your daily 8 glasses of fluid): ½ cup (125ml) juice is equal to one serving of fruit. Remember, however, that being a concentrated fruit also means juices are generally a concentrated source of kilojoules; it can take up to three apples to make just one glass of juice, and many fruits contain a high level of natural sugars.

WHEN CALCULATING 8 GLASSES OF WATER A DAY, CAN YOU INCLUDE TEA, COFFEE AND OTHER FLUIDS?

Yes, your daily fluid intake doesn't all have to come in the form of water. While water is best, milk, juice, tea, coffee, cordial, soft drinks, sports drinks, even ice-blocks, can also provide additional fluids.

Alcohol, on the other hand, has a diuretic effect (increases the production of urine), and should be accompanied with a glass of water to prevent dehydration.

And don't forget food. Some foods contain high amounts of fluid; custard, jelly, ice-cream, soup and broth all add to your daily fluid intake.

Don't forget, you need to drink more fluids if it is a hot day, you are doing strenuous activity or are ill, to prevent dehydration.

WE'RE TRYING TO BE MORE HEALTHY IN OUR HOUSE. HOW CAN WE BEST GET OUR DAILY 2 AND 5 SERVINGS OF FRUIT AND VEGETABLES, AND WHAT IS A SERVING EQUAL TO?

According to the Government *Go for 2&5* campaign, one serving of vegetables is equal to 1 cup salad vegetables, ½ cup cooked vegetables, or ½ cup cooked legumes (dried peas, beans or lentils).

One serving of fruit is equal to ½ cup fresh fruit juice, 1 cup canned or chopped fruit, 1 medium-sized piece (e.g. apple, pear, orange), 2 smaller pieces (e.g. apricot, kiwifruit) or 1½ tablespoons dried fruit.

It's easy to increase your daily fruit and vegetable servings, just top your breakfast cereal with some chopped fruit or have a fruit smoothie. Try snacking on a piece of fruit instead of a biscuit and have a fruit salad for dessert.

Try a salad with lunch, add more vegetables to your stir-fry or casserole, and add a variety of grated vegetables to the basic mixture to make a delicious savoury pancake or omelette.

COOKING FOR CROWDS

Planning a party

A party checklist

Tripling recipes for crowds

What to feed the football team

I AM PLANNING AN ENGAGEMENT PARTY FOR 16 PEOPLE. I'VE NOT DONE ANYTHING LIKE THIS BEFORE. ANY TIPS FOR A FIRST TIMER?

PARTY CHECKLISTS

A party calls for four checklists:

1. A **detailed menu** listing all the food and drink plus all the incidentals – accompaniments such as dipping sauces for Asian appetisers and breads or other items to go with dips, garnishes and ice and lemon slices or other items to go into drinks.

2. Preparation and assembly time Go back over the first list and note what you need in the way of bench space for putting final touches on the food and for filling serving platters. How much time in the oven and/or space in the fridge and freezer will each item on the menu need? Make a list of the best order in which to serve them so you won't have to heat several things in the oven, or grill or fry them at the same time. Make a big copy of this "running list" to be taped up in the kitchen on the day of the party, so that both you and any helpers will know what to do next. Decide where you will have the bar, whether behind the scenes or in the party space, and consider how to organise it.

3. An equipment checklist What you need to hire or borrow, from extra cutlery to a marquee plus fans to cool it or heaters to warm it. Shop around before hiring; the variations in prices can be quite amazing. Here is a list to help you – photocopy it, then insert your own numbers; change it as you need.

- cutlery
- serving platters, bowls, baskets and trays
- bowls for toothpicks, olive stones, etc.
- airtight food storage containers
- glassware
- cups and saucers
- plates
- coasters
- tea- and coffee-making equipment and serving pots, jugs and sugar bowls
- bar equipment and ice supply
- napkins – allow three times the number of guests

- oven trays
- extra appliances such as hotplates and warmers
- insulated boxes plus cold bricks to supplement the fridge in keeping food cold
- chairs
- music equipment
- flowers or decorations
- tea-towels
- disposable washcloths
- hand towels and toilet paper for the bathrooms
- garbage bins
- marquee
- fans or heaters

4. A plan of action or "running list", should be started weeks before a big party and at least one week before a small one. It should list everything you have to do from inviting the guests to hiring equipment, shopping, cooking, setting up the bar, decorating and organising the party space, and last-minute chores on the day such as doing the flowers or collecting ice. Put the tasks in order and assign each one to a day, counting down to the day of the party. If it all looks too much, this is the time to consider it calmly and cut down, simplify or delegate to reliable helpers until it is manageable.

A MONTH BEFORE

Work out the guest numbers considering budget, space limitations and how hard you want to work.

Send out invitations that not only state the address, date and time of the party, but also clearly indicate what guests can expect in terms of being fed and watered: inviting people at mealtime then passing a few simple hors d'oeuvres could strain the friendship. Include an RSVP date on the invitation too, so you'll be confident of your numbers.

Start menu-planning. You don't have to make something for everyone, but do look after guests with dietary restrictions and vegetarians.

Decide if you're having pre-dinner nibbles (4-5 pieces of food per person per hour) with drinks; a full-on cocktail party (4-5 pieces of food per person for the first hour then 4 pieces of food for each hour after that); or the equivalent of a whole meal (12-14 fairly substantial pieces of food served throughout the duration of the event). It's a good idea to choose a variety of hot and cold savouries. Put together a list of recipes that spans a wide spectrum of foods, checking they don't all require the same preparation or assembly time.

3 WEEKS BEFORE

Create a checklist, working three weeks backwards from the party date on a calendar. Start planning and decide what chores can be done two weeks before, one week before, a few days before and on the day of the party.

Place orders for flowers; book a bartender, a chef and/or wait-staff if you're hosting a crowd; look into party-hire now, too, if it's required. Tables, chairs, glassware, cutlery, china, linen, a marquee and the like, aren't easy to get at a moment's notice.

2 WEEKS BEFORE

Finalise the menu then make your shopping list; make separate lists for soft drinks and mixers, wines and spirits, supermarket items and whatever else is on the game plan – butcher, greengrocer, deli, etc.

Go through your cocktail equipment, making sure you have everything you need in terms of glassware, mixers, bar tools and accessories (salt, sugar, soda water, lime juice, bitters, etc). Buy your drink requirements, pantry ingredients, non-perishable decorating items, and any extra serving equipment you need.

1 WEEK BEFORE

Check out your serving trays, platters and bowls and decide what food is to go on or into what dish.

Finalise the shopping list, dividing it into ingredients for canapés that can be purchased, prepared and refrigerated in advance, and those that shouldn't be purchased until closer to party time. Some of the food can be made and frozen now, while other dishes' bases or accompaniments can be prepared and kept under refrigeration until it's time to complete the recipes.

It's a good idea now, when you're thinking of the overall plan, to write a list that spells out the "running" order of food preparation and presentation, in detail, on the day.

2 DAYS BEFORE

Clean the house, verandah and garden area thoroughly, and begin to put the party area together. Wash and dry cutlery, glasses and serving platters or trays that haven't seen the light of day for ages. Leave them, covered with tea-towels or any clean cloth, out of the way somewhere near the kitchen or bar. Set up the bar – spirits, wines, liqueurs, blenders, cocktail shakers and the glasses.

1 DAY BEFORE

Arrange to have any hired equipment, flowers, cases of beer and/or soft drinks, etc., delivered or pick them up yourself.

Finish any remaining grocery shopping – leave the herbs and other fresh items for this trip. Make any food that can hold safely until the party starts.

PARTY DAY

Early in the day, purchase enough ice to chill the drinks *and* have sufficient quantities left over for the cocktails – you can never have too much ice. Try storing ice and drinks inside your dishwasher: the melted ice drains away and the drinks remain cold. A laundry tub or a child's wading pool are also good containers for keeping drinks on ice.

Finish cooking as much as you can before anyone arrives so you don't have to spend most of the party in your kitchen. Plate whatever food you can in advance.

Make cocktails and other drinks for guests on arrival, and show them where they can help themselves to refills if you don't have a bartender.

It could be said that most of your enjoyment of the party will depend on how successful it is, and this relates to how well you've planned ahead and how easily everything falls into place once the guests start arriving.

See page 106 for a guide to the number of food and drinks required depending on guest numbers.

Here's a rough guide of how many varieties of food and drink you'll need at your next party, depending on how many guests. The numbers are based on a 2-hour cocktail party.

NO. OF GUESTS	8	15	25	35	50
DIPS	2	2	2	3	3
COLD FINGER FOOD	2	3	3	4	5
HOT FINGER FOOD	2	3	3	4	5
WINE (750ML BOTTLES)	4	7	12	17	25
COCKTAILS	2	2	3	3	4
SOFT DRINKS (2-LITRE BOTTLES)	4	4	4	4	4

MY FAMILY IS COMING FOR A HEARTY CASSEROLE. THERE WILL ONLY BE 12 OF US; CAN I SIMPLY TRIPLE MY FAMOUS RECIPE, WHICH NORMALLY SERVES FOUR?

This is one of our most commonly asked questions, and there isn't a straight yes or no answer. Most households don't have large pots and pans, so large quantities of casseroles and the like tend to get pushed into the pan you'd usually use for making one quantity.

Most casserole recipes start by browning the meat for good flavour and colour, and this must be done properly. If you try and brown too much meat at the one time, it will turn grey, lose its juiciness and will toughen. So, either use larger pots and pans, or make the recipe in the usually smaller quantities until you have enough to serve 12.

I'M HAVING A VERY CASUAL OUTDOOR PARTY FOR 20 BIG BURLY FOOTBALLERS. WHAT DO YOU SUGGEST I SERVE IN THE WAY OF FOOD? THEY'RE BRINGING THEIR OWN DRINKS. IT WILL BE HELD IN THE EVENING WHEN THE WEATHER IS QUITE COOL.

We get the picture. How about three hearty pasta-based recipes. It's best to serve the hot sauces and pasta in separate bowls. If you mix the sauces through the pasta, it will soon soak up the sauce and won't be nearly as good.

Make sure you make a bolognaise sauce – most people love it – and have a large bowl of grated parmesan cheese ready for the topping. A creamy seafood sauce, particularly prawn, will always be popular; have a bowl of chopped parsley and green onion – or whatever suits the recipe – for sprinkling on top. The third sauce could be a tomato-based chicken sauce, or maybe a vegetable sauce such as a ratatouille. Don't forget lots of crusty bread, but forget the salads, they probably won't be touched.

If you prefer, make it a curry party – once again, keep the hot sauces and rice in separate bowls. Make sure you have one hot, one medium and one mild curry – to please everyone. There are lots of simple accompaniments you can have with curries, such as pickles, chutneys, yogurt, cucumber, dried fruit, and lime and lemon wedges. And, don't forget the bread – there are plenty of Indian-style breads available in supermarkets.

FRUIT & VEGETABLES

Opening fresh coconuts

Getting the most juice from citrus fruits

How to quickly ripen fruit

Peeling garlic & capsicum

Roasting the perfect potato

MY HUSBAND CAME HOME WITH A FRESH COCONUT. HOW DO I OPEN IT?

Pierce the softest eye of the coconut with a sturdy metal skewer. Place it on an oven tray and heat in a preheated hot oven (220°C/200°C fan-forced) for 10 minutes. Leave it to cool. It should split of its own accord, although it might need a bit of a tap. The shell will separate easily from the flesh.

I HAVE HEARD YOU CAN WARM CITRUS FRUIT IN THE MICROWAVE OVEN TO GET MORE JUICE – IS THIS TRUE?

Yes, heat them for about 10 seconds on HIGH (100%) before squeezing them. Another way is to roll the fruit back and forth on a flat surface, pressing firmly, to make juicing easier.

WHAT IS A POMELO?

A pomelo is similar to a grapefruit but sweeter, somewhat more conical in shape and slightly larger, about the size of a small coconut. The firm rind peels away easily and neatly, like a mandarin, and the segments are easy to separate.

I'VE HEARD THAT YOU CAN GET UNRIPE FRUIT TO RIPEN QUICKER BY PLACING IT IN A BROWN PAPER BAG. HOW DOES THIS WORK?

The reason some fruits ripen when placed in a bag is because they give off ethylene gas, which is known to ripen some fruit. Ethylene is responsible for the ripening of tomatoes, peaches, apples and the sprouting of potatoes.

Bananas give off a lot of ethylene, and is often the fruit of choice to place in the bag with unripened fruit to speed up the ripening process.

IS GREEN PAPAYA SIMPLY UNRIPE PAPAYA? I CAN'T FIND IT AT MY GREENGROCER OR SUPERMARKET. WHERE DO YOU BUY IT?

Yes, green papayas are just unripe papayas. They are available at Asian food stores; look for one that is hard and slightly shiny, proving it is freshly picked. It's important that it is totally unripe – the flesh so light green it's almost white – it has more crunch than flavour, and it acts as a sponge to absorb the combined hot, sour, sweet and salty Thai flavours in salads. Green papaya will ripen rapidly if not used within a day or two.

IS THERE AN EASY WAY TO PEEL GARLIC?

To remove the skin from a garlic clove easily without having it stick to your fingers, smash each clove with the side of a large, heavy knife. Remove the skin. Another solid whack on the clove will crush the garlic sufficiently to be used.

HOW DO I REMOVE THE SKIN FROM A CAPSICUM?

Quarter the capsicum and remove the seeds and membranes. Roast under a grill or in a very hot oven, skin-side up, until the skin blisters and blackens. Cover capsicum pieces with paper or plastic wrap (or put into a plastic bag or under an upside-down bowl) for 5 minutes then peel away the skin and cut into thick strips, as required.

Another easy method is to roast the capsicum pieces on a simmer mat over a gas flame. (A simmer mat, also known as a heat diffuser, sits on top of the hot plate and helps control the temperature of the cooking surface.)

A whole capsicum can be placed on an oven tray and roasted at 220°C/200° fan-forced until the skin is blistered and blackened, turning once. Cover and stand, as before.

HOW DO I CORRECTLY PEEL AND SEED A TOMATO?

Cut a shallow cross in the base of the tomato and place in a heatproof bowl. Cover with boiling water and stand about 30 seconds then remove the tomato with a slotted spoon. Peel away skin from the cut end.

To seed a tomato, cut it in half crossways and squeeze gently to remove the seeds. Or, cut into wedges and scrape out the seeds with a small spoon.

CAN YOU RIPEN TOMATOES THAT HAVE BEEN PICKED GREEN?

Tomatoes should be ripened at room temperature, in mildly warm temperatures away from direct sunlight. When fully ripe, especially in hot weather, they may be stored in the refrigerator for several days. However, they will gradually lose flavour and some soft areas may develop in the flesh. Bring to room temperature before eating.

ARE BEETROOT LEAVES EDIBLE? IF SO, CAN THEY BE EATEN BOTH RAW AND COOKED?

Beetroot leaves are edible. Many chefs include beetroot leaf recipes in their cookbooks and most recommend eating the more tender young leaves, as the older leaves taste bitter. They can be served raw in salads dressed with balsamic vinegar; partially cooked by being tossed with just-drained hot pasta; or braised with butter or olive oil in a covered frying pan. If you intend to eat the leaves, separate them from the bulbs and store them, wrapped, in the refrigerator for no more than two or three days.

HOW DO I COOK FRESH BEETROOT?

Prepare fresh beetroot by scrubbing the outside (rather than peeling it). Trim any foliage, but do not cut into the beet itself as this will cause bleeding when it cooks. Don't trim the beard at the base of the plant, and leave at least 2cm length of stem on the vegetable to stop it from bleeding.

To boil beetroot, add whole beets to boiling water and cook for about 45 minutes, depending on their size. A skewer should slide through the thickest part easily to indicate it is cooked. Cool for 10 minutes, then peel with a vegetable peeler or, simply split and squeeze the skin with gloved hands, the skin should slip off easily.

To roast whole beetroot, wrap in foil and roast at 180°C/160°C fan-forced for about 45 minutes, depending on how large they are. Or chop coarsely, toss in olive oil and fresh thyme leaves and roast at 200°C/180°C fan-forced for about 30 minutes or until tender.

To microwave, peel and chop beetroot and microwave according to the manufacturer's instructions (about 20-30 minutes).

MY PUMPKIN ALWAYS SEEMS TO GO MOULDY. HOW DO I STOP THIS HAPPENING?

Pumpkins aren't the only vegetable that is prone to mould; it also happens frequently to marrows, squash and onions. To reduce mould growth, store at room temperature under dry conditions.

IS IT TRUE THAT POTATOES THAT HAVE GONE GREEN ARE POISONOUS? CAN YOU USE ANY PART OF A GREEN POTATO?

Our advice is that any potato with green patches should be avoided; the greening may indicate that the potato harbours toxins produced by over exposure to sunlight. They can also taste bitter.

HOW CAN I ROAST THE PERFECT POTATO? MINE ARE NEVER LOVELY AND CRISP.

Perfectly roasted potatoes should be crisp and golden brown on the outside, and densely smooth and moist on the inside; full-flavoured and rich but never greasy. Olive oil is better to brush potatoes with than any other oil or butter because it tolerates high oven temperatures and gives a pleasant taste to the potatoes. Gently raking along the length of the partly-cooked surface of the potato with the tines of a fork assists in crisping.

It's important to use an oven tray with shallow sides – about 1cm – this allows the oven heat to brown the potatoes. Potatoes roasted in deep-sided baking dishes simply don't brown well enough. Don't crowd potatoes on the oven tray because they will brown unevenly, and make certain the oven has reached the correct temperature before the tray goes in. Varieties good for roasting are pontiac, desiree, lasoda and kipfler.

PERFECT ROAST POTATOES

Preheat the oven to 220°C/200°C fan-forced. Peel and halve six medium potatoes; boil, steam or microwave until they are beginning to cook. As a guide, put the potatoes into a saucepan, barely cover them with cold water, cover the pan then bring the potatoes to the boil. If the potato pieces are small to medium, this will be enough cooking. If they're large, then simmer the potatoes for 3-5 minutes. Steaming potatoes will work with similar timing to boiling. If you want to par-cook potatoes in a microwave oven, allow about 30 seconds for each potato half – cook on HIGH (100%).

Drain potatoes; pat dry with absorbent paper. Rake rounded sides of potato halves gently with a fork; place halves, cut-side down, on a lightly oiled oven tray. Brush potatoes all over with olive oil before roasting, uncovered, for about 50 minutes or until browned and crisp all over. There is no need to turn the potatoes.

IS THERE A QUICKER WAY TO ROAST POTATOES? THEY ALWAYS SEEM TO TAKE SO LONG TO COOK.

Pour enough oil into a shallow-sided oven tray to barely cover the base of the tray; put the tray into a cold oven. Preheat the oven to the hottest setting while you are preparing the potatoes.

Peel and halve potatoes, then microwave (or boil or steam) until they are cooked through. Dry potatoes then roughly score the outside with a fork (or just roughly shake in a colander). Once the oven has reached the correct temperature, remove the oven tray and add the potatoes. The trick here is that the oil has to be very hot before the potatoes are added. Return the oven tray and potatoes to the oven, then reduce the oven temperature to 200°C/180°C fan-forced; cook until the potatoes are golden brown, about 25 minutes.

MY POTATO SALAD OFTEN TURNS TO MUSH. WHERE AM I GOING WRONG?

The mushiness is usually caused by the potatoes being over crowded in the pan and during draining and cooling. About 1kg of halved baby potatoes will be fine in a medium saucepan. Put the potatoes into a half-filled pan of boiling salted water; cover, return to the boil (or steam) then simmer until the potatoes are almost tender. Gently drain potatoes into a large strainer (so the potatoes underneath are not crushed). Quickly spread the potatoes onto a tray in a single layer; they will continue to cook in their own heat.

I HAVE A CASSEROLE RECIPE THAT ASKS FOR A MIREPOIX. WHAT IS IT?

Mirepoix (meer-pwah) is a French term used to describe a mixture of diced carrots, onions and celery (sometimes also herbs, ham or lean bacon) sautéed in butter or oil. It is used to enhance the flavour base for sauces, soups and stews, and can also be used as a bed to braise meat and fish.

HERBS & SPICES

The difference between herbs & spices

Storing fresh herbs

Using ginger, coriander & lemon grass

Using certain spices

Why some spices are heated

WHAT'S THE DIFFERENCE BETWEEN HERBS AND SPICES?

These days the distinction is a little blurry, but generally herbs are the fragrant leaves of plants that do not have woody stems, such as parsley, thyme, peppermint, whereas spices are obtained from plant roots, flowers, fruits, seeds and bark.

CAN I SUBSTITUTE DRY HERBS FOR FRESH?

As a rough guide, dried (not ground) herbs can be used in the proportion of one to four, i.e., use 1 teaspoon dried herbs instead of 4 teaspoons (1 tablespoon) chopped fresh herbs, however, this depends on the actual recipe and the pungency and freshness of both dried and fresh herbs.

I HAVE LOTS OF HERBS GROWING IN MY GARDEN AND LIKE TO USE THEM IN MY COOKING. IS THERE A WAY OF PRESERVING THEM?

Wash and dry herbs thoroughly then blend or process them with a little olive oil. Freeze small amounts, flattened, in plastic bags or ice-cube trays. When solid, pop out the cubes and store them in a plastic freezer bag or airtight container.

WHAT IS A BOUQUET GARNI AND WHERE CAN I BUY IT?

Bouquet garni is a bunch of aromatic herbs used to flavour sauces, stews, soups, casseroles and stocks. It generally consists of parsley, thyme and bay leaves, which are tied together using unwaxed kitchen string, or enclosed in a small muslin bag. The herbs are removed from the dish before serving. You can make your own by tying together 2-3 sprigs fresh parsley, 1 sprig fresh thyme and 1-2 fresh or dried bay leaves.

A LOT OF ASIAN RECIPES ASK FOR CORIANDER ROOT AND STEM MIXTURE. WHAT IS THIS? CAN I USE GROUND CORIANDER INSTEAD?

When fresh, coriander is also known as pak chee, cilantro or chinese parsley. It is a bright-green-leafed herb with a pungent flavour. The whole coriander plant is used in Thai cooking to impart a stronger flavour to some dishes. This is why, when you buy a bunch of coriander, it is one of the very few fresh herbs that comes with its stems and roots intact.

Wash the stems and roots well then scrape the roots with a small flat knife to remove some of the outer fibrous skin. Finely or coarsely chop the roots and stems and reserve the amount required for the recipe. Any leftover root and stem mixture can be frozen in teaspoon-sized parcels wrapped in plastic-wrap.

Coriander is also available ground or as seeds; these should not be substituted for fresh coriander as the tastes are completely different.

WHAT IS THE DIFFERENCE BETWEEN SEA SALT AND ROCK SALT, AND IN WHAT INSTANCE SHOULD YOU USE EACH?

Rock salt is the lowest grade salt you can buy – you would use it as a cooling agent only (salt lowers the freezing point of ice, so it absorbs heat from anything around it, keeping things cooler for longer). It is the sort of salt you see your oysters served on. It is very strong in flavour and completely unrefined.

Sea salt flakes are harvested from salt plains (evaporated sea water) and have a much more subtle flavour. It includes very small amounts of other minerals, so you can't really use it for preserving as the minerals will discolour the food. It is the best salt to use on the dinner table as a last minute seasoning for food. It is also good to cook with.

HOW MUCH OF THE LEMON GRASS PLANT CAN BE EATEN? TRIMMED GREEN-WHITE STALKS ARE SOLD AT THE SHOPS, BUT I NEVER SEE THEM WITH THEIR BRIGHT GREEN TOPS – CAN THEY BE EATEN, TOO?

In Australia we seldom use the green blade-like tops, but there's no reason you can't use the whole blade as a flavouring when cooking, just as you do kaffir lime or bay leaves, removing them before serving the dish. The blade adds a sharp, citrusy flavour and works well with chilli and coconut.

In Thailand, the blade is used, sliced extremely finely against the grain, in various seafood and grilled meat salads. In Vietnam, the green tops are soaked in water, which is then chilled and served over ice with some of their more incendiary dishes – sort of an Asian version of lemonade.

In Australia, however, we usually just slice the bulb section thinly, then cut the slices into minuscule pieces to use in sauces, dressings and marinades, stir-fries and most Asian soups. If chopped finely enough, lemon grass is especially good sprinkled with fresh chilli over grilled fish or other seafood.

I TASTED ZA'ATAR FOR THE FIRST TIME THE OTHER DAY. WHAT IS IT?

Za'atar is a blend of roasted dried spices and usually includes wild marjoram, thyme, sumac and sesame seeds. It's available from Middle-Eastern food shops, delicatessens and some supermarkets. Za'atar is sprinkled over many Middle-Eastern dishes including meat, vegetables and pitta bread.

You can make your own za'atar by combining 1 tablespoon sumac, 1 tablespoon roasted sesame seeds, 1 teaspoon dried marjoram and 2 teaspoons dried thyme. Keep what you don't use, stored in a glass jar with a tight-fitting lid, in the fridge for up to three months.

I HAVE NOTICED MANY RECIPES CALL FOR EITHER SWEET, HOT OR SMOKED PAPRIKA – WHAT IS THE DIFFERENCE BETWEEN THEM?

The word paprika is actually a derivation of the Latin word for pepper, "piper", and the spice is from one of the many fruits belonging to the capsicum species. Hungarians grow more than 40 variations of the varieties of capsicum fruit used to form paprika. Each of the six Hungarian paprika types (fiery hot, hot, medium sharp, semi-sweet, sweet and exquisite delicate) is produced from a different permutation of the capsicum.

Spain grows a particular type of large, round capsicum called a pimentón that can be sun-dried or smoked before being ground. It is sold as three individual paprikas – dulce (sweet), agridulce (semi-sweet) and picante (spicy hot).

As for usage, the sweeter or more delicately flavoured paprikas are used mainly for colouring with just a hint of flavour while the heat of a spicy paprika is for the cook who likes this flavourful seasoning to dominate the dish.

WHAT IS SUMAC?

Sumac is a purple-red, astringent spice ground from berries growing on shrubs that flourish wild around the Mediterranean. It adds a tart, lemony flavour to dips and dressings, and goes well with barbecued meat. Sumac can be found in Middle-Eastern food stores and some supermarkets.

I HAVE A NUMBER OF ENGLISH RECIPES THAT USE MACE, WHICH I HAVE BEEN UNABLE TO FIND. IS THERE A SUBSTITUTE?

Mace is the fine, bright red membrane that covers the nutmeg seed. It is very similar in flavour, though is slightly more pungent. Ground nutmeg can be substituted for ground mace.

121

I AM NOT SURE HOW TO USE FRESH GINGER IN COOKING. SHOULD I PEEL IT BEFORE USING?

Ginger is a plant from tropical and subtropical regions. It is grown for its root, which is the part you buy in the shop.

Much of the flavour of ginger is just under the skin, so if you can avoid peeling it before using then that is better. The best way to do so is to scrape at the skin with a teaspoon rather than using a vegetable peeler (however, you may find using a peeler is easier).

Ginger can be used in both sweet and savoury dishes and goes well with a great number of other flavours. It is fantastic with white fish, in Asian recipes and stir-fries, as well as steeped in boiling water to make a soothing tea.

Thinly scrape off the outer skin then grate, or cut into matchstick-size pieces, for a more intense flavour. Only a little is required, usually a 2cm or 3cm piece, grated, is enough ginger for a recipe.

Ground ginger, also known as powdered ginger, is used as a flavouring in cakes, pies and puddings but cannot be substituted for fresh ginger.

ARE ALLSPICE AND MIXED SPICE THE SAME THING?

No, allspice, also known as pimento or jamaican pepper, is a berry, so-named because it tastes like a combination of cinnamon, nutmeg, cumin and cloves – all spices. The berries, dark brown in colour and about the size of a pea, are the dried, unripe fruits of a tropical evergreen tree native to Jamaica. It can be used in both sweet and savoury dishes and is available ground or whole. Ground allspice should not be confused with mixed spice, which is much milder and sweeter in flavour.

Mixed spice is a classic mixture containing cumin, caraway, allspice, coriander, nutmeg and ginger, although cinnamon and other spices can be added. It is used in sweet dishes such as fruit cakes, fruit pies, biscuits and a lot of sweet, baked items.

HOW DO YOU USE A VANILLA BEAN POD?

To use a vanilla bean pod, cut the bean in half lengthwise and scrape out the seeds and pulp; add this, along with the pod, to the liquid and stand for the specified time. The pods can then be removed. Wash the pods in cool water, dry them thoroughly, then put them into a container where you store sugar (usually caster sugar) for baking. This way, you'll always have vanilla-flavoured sugar on hand.

Some recipes call for whole pods, in this case the pods can be washed in cool water after use, dried thoroughly and used again.

WHAT IS STAR ANISE AND WHAT IS IT USED FOR?

Star anise is the dried, star-shaped seed pod of a small evergreen tree grown from Indochina to Japan. Both the pod and seeds have a slight licorice taste, more spicily pungent than anise, with overtones of clove and cinnamon.

It is an ingredient in the classic chinese five-spice blend that incorporates sweet, sour, bitter, pungent and salty tastes, by combining star anise, fennel, clove, cinnamon, and black or sichuan pepper.

It's used to flavour teas, broths, rich stews, tangy dressings and sweet syrups. Use star anise sparingly, as it's very aromatic. It keeps well, if stored whole, in an airtight container.

WHY DO YOU HAVE TO COOK THE SPICE PASTE OR SPICES FOR CURRIES INSTEAD OF JUST ADDING THEM TO THE MAIN INGREDIENTS?

Many spices need to be ground, roasted, toasted or fried to release their flavours. Just as garlic and onions release their natural aromas when we fry them, volatile oils are released from spices, which enhances or intensifies their flavour, or can even bring out a whole different flavour characteristic.

FOOD STORAGE

How to store baked goods

Storing meat, chicken & seafood

Keeping your fridge in good condition

Freezing food safely

Storing dried foods

Shelf life of fresh fruit & vegies

WHAT IS THE BEST WAY TO STORE BISCUITS AND SLICES?

Cool biscuits and slices before storing – if you store them warm, they will become soft. Store in an airtight container, leaving minimal air space.

Biscuits that need to be filled should be stored unfilled and assembled just before serving; if the filling is baked in, they are best eaten the same day. Don't store biscuits with cake or bread as these will soften the biscuits.

If unfilled and un-iced biscuits become soft, they can be re-crisped by placing in a single layer on oven trays and heating in a moderate oven (180°C/160°C fan-forced) for 5 to 10 minutes – check often as they will overbrown quickly. Transfer to wire racks to cool.

Don't store biscuits and slices for too long – even in airtight containers they gradually become stale and limp after about a week.

CAN I FREEZE BISCUITS?

Biscuits can be frozen for three months. Freeze cooled un-iced or unfilled biscuits in an airtight container, using sheets of freezer film between the layers. Frozen iced or cream-filled biscuits may crack or change in appearance on thawing.

CAN I FREEZE SCONES?

Scones freeze well. To freeze uncooked scones, leave them in the pan or on the oven tray to freeze, then place them in freezer bags expelling as much air as possible. Mark the bags with a use-by-date, which, so long as you've made them airtight, should be about two months after making. To bake uncooked scones, remove from the freezer bag and cook in a hot oven (220°C/200°C fan-forced) for about 20 minutes.

To freeze cooked scones, place cold scones in a freezer bag and expel as much air as possible. Freeze for up to two months. To reheat, remove scones from the bag, wrap in foil and reheat in a moderate oven (180°C/160°C fan-forced) for about 20 minutes.

HOW LONG WILL FRIANDS KEEP?

Friands are best eaten the day they are made, but can be stored in an airtight container for up to two days. They can be frozen for up to two months, but nothing beats freshly baked friands.

HOW LONG WILL A WHITE CHOCOLATE MUD CAKE KEEP?

White chocolate mud cakes keep particularly well because of the high sugar and fat content. Small cakes will become staler faster than large cakes due to the smaller surface area. Mud cakes will keep at room temperature in an airtight container for at least a week; longer in the fridge and for several months in the freezer.

HOW LONG WILL DRIED YEAST LAST?

Dried yeast is usually packed in boxes of sealed foil sachets containing 7g (3 teaspoons) each. Store in the fridge, where it should keep indefinitely.

LAST SUMMER, OUR PASSIONFRUIT VINES GAVE AN ABUNDANCE OF FRUIT. I'VE GIVEN AWAY BAGS TO FRIENDS AND MADE MANY DISHES CONTAINING PASSIONFRUIT, BUT IS THERE A WAY TO FREEZE THE FRUIT FOR LATER USE?

Passionfruit freezes well, so for year-round supplies, just scoop out the pulp and freeze it in ice-cube trays or small containers. When solid, pop out the cubes and store them in a plastic freezer bag or airtight container for use at a minute's notice.

Fresh passionfruit to be used within a week can be stored in a plastic bag in the fridge. Passionfruit will dehydrate quickly if kept at room temperature.

WHAT IS THE BEST WAY TO STORE MUFFINS?

Muffins are at their best if eaten fresh from the oven while they are still warm. However, they can be kept in an airtight container for up to two days and frozen for up to three months.

Place the cold muffins in a freezer bag or wrap individually in plastic wrap or foil (depending on how you intend to reheat them), expelling as much air as possible by wrapping as tightly as possible or pressing the bag gently.

To thaw muffins, reheat foil-wrapped muffins by placing them in a single layer on an oven tray, and reheating at 180°C/160°C fan-forced for about 20 minutes or until they are heated through.

You can thaw muffins in a microwave oven, but as ovens vary in power, we can only give general guidelines for timing. Reheat plastic-wrapped muffins, one at a time, on MEDIUM LOW (30%). Allow about 45 seconds for one muffin. Err on the conservative side with timing. You can always put them back in the microwave for a further short burst. Defrosted muffins should not feel hot to the touch. If they do, they are probably overheated and will toughen as they cool.

HOW DO I BEST STORE A CAKE?

Most cakes will keep well for two or three days depending on the climate and type of cake; as a rule, remember that the higher the fat content, the longer a cake keeps.

Cool the cake to room temperature before storing it in an airtight container as close in size to the cake as possible to minimise the amount of air around the cake.

For a cake that is suitable to freeze, it is usually better to do so unfilled and un-iced because icing can crack during the thawing process. A cake thaws best overnight in the refrigerator. Wrap or seal the cake in freezer wrap or freezer bags, expelling as much air as possible.

WHAT IS THE BEST WAY TO STORE UNFILLED CHOUX PASTRIES?

Cool pastries completely before storing. They keep well in airtight containers, but after a week or so they gradually lose their shape and texture, so it is best to freeze them if you want to keep them for longer.

WHAT IS THE BEST WAY TO STORE A SPONGE CAKE?

Sponges are best made and eaten on the day of serving. Unfilled sponges can be frozen for up to one month; place in a freezer bag and expel as much air as possible before placing in the freezer.

HOW DO I STORE MY FRUIT CAKE?

When the cake is cold, remove it from the pan, leaving the lining paper intact; wrap the cake tightly in plastic wrap, then in aluminium foil. It can then be stored in a cool, dry place for up to six months, or in the refrigerator for up to a year or frozen indefinitely in a container to protect it.

If there is a danger of the cake being discovered by insects, then the refrigerator (or freezer) is the best place to keep it.

Humidity can be a problem (causing mould), but if the cake is rich in sugar and fruit, and stored correctly, it should keep indefinitely.

We prefer to store a rich fruit cake in the refrigerator simply because it will cut better; once sliced, it quickly returns to room temperature.

PATTY CAKES SEEM TO GO STALE QUICKLY. WHY IS THIS?

Patty cakes (or cupcakes) have only a small surface area, so they go stale much faster than larger cakes. They are best eaten on the day they're baked, or frozen – they thaw quite fast at room temperature.

HOW DO I STORE A DECORATED FRUIT CAKE AND HOW LONG WILL IT KEEP?

Cakes will keep well if they have been correctly covered with almond icing and fondant. They need to be protected from moisture in the air – either rain or humidity or, worse, both. If possible, keep the cake in a cabinet or under glass or plastic so you can check for changes in the cake's appearance.

If the surface of the cake becomes wet and sticky, remove the cake from the cabinet and stand it under an ordinary reading lamp (not fluorescent). Turn the cake every now and then until the fondant looks and feels dry, then return it to the cabinet.

Decorated cakes can be frozen if they are to be kept for more than three months. Put the cake in a plastic container, leaving as little air space around the cake and its decorations as possible. Thaw the cake, covered, in the refrigerator. This process will take up to two days.

CAN I FREEZE LEFTOVER PASTRY?

Pastry can be stored, wrapped tightly in plastic wrap or a plastic bag, in the refrigerator for one or two days, or frozen for up to a month. When freezing, be sure to label with a use-by date.

To defrost, stand the pastry overnight in the refrigerator and return to room temperature before rolling. You can also freeze lined unbaked pastry cases. Thaw overnight in the refrigerator.

HOW DO I KEEP FRESH BERRIES?

Don't wash berries before storing. Place berries in a single layer on an absorbent-paper-lined tray or plate – this helps to absorb moisture. Cover loosely with plastic wrap and keep refrigerated for up to two days.

HOW DO YOU STORE FRESHLY CUT HERBS?

The best way to keep fresh herbs is to stand them in a jar of water, refreshing the water every second day. Place a plastic bag over the top, securing it to the jar with a rubber band and keep in the fridge. They should last about a week if stored this way.

WHAT IS THE BEST WAY TO STORE SPICES?

Spices can be stored in an airtight container in a cool, dry, dark place, or in the freezer. Spices lose their aroma and flavour over time.

WHAT IS THE BEST WAY TO STORE NUTS?

Due to the high fat content in nuts they can go rancid very quickly. Light, heat and moisture will spoil nuts. Store them in sealed plastic bags or containers in a dark, cool, dry place or in the fridge or freezer. They will keep for up to three months in the fridge and six months in the freezer.

HOW DO I FREEZE BACON?

Divide bacon rashers into pairs; wrap in plastic wrap, folding in the ends to completely enclose. Freeze wrapped pairs in a large snap-lock plastic bag for up to three months. To use, remove only as many bundles of two rashers as you need. They'll defrost quickly and there is no waste.

CAN CREAM BE FROZEN?

If you use frozen then defrosted cream in a recipe where the cream is to be poured or heated, then that is fine. However, defrosted cream won't whip.

HOW LONG WILL MY CHRISTMAS HAM KEEP?

When stored correctly, you can keep ham for up to 10 days. Dip a clean large tea-towel or an old clean pillowcase in a solution of two cups water and 1 tablespoon white vinegar. Squeeze out and wrap the ham in the tea-towel or place in the pillowcase. Re-dip the tea-towel or pillowcase in the vinegar solution every two days and change or wash the tea-towel or pillowcase at least once during storage. Store ham in the coldest part of the fridge.

CAN I FREEZE HOMEMADE SAUSAGE ROLLS BEFORE COOKING THEM?

Yes, after you've rolled the pastry around the mince mixture, wrap the long roll in the piece of plastic that keeps the frozen pastry sheets apart. Stack the long rolls in an airtight container with as little air space as possible, and freeze for up to three months.

When it's time to cook the rolls, take the number of rolls you need out of the container, put them on a wire rack in a single layer to thaw (rolls can also be thawed overnight in the refrigerator).

Preheat the oven to 220°C/200°C fan-forced, and line the oven trays with baking paper. Glaze the rolls, then make cuts in the tops of the rolls for the steam to escape. Cut the long rolls into the size you want, pop the sausage rolls on the trays and cook for about 30 minutes or until browned.

IS IT TRUE COOKED MEAT DISHES SHOULD BE PLACED IN THE FRIDGE TO COOL, AND NOT LEFT ON THE BENCH TOP?

Yes. Meat, poultry and seafood should be refrigerated as soon as possible after cooking and not left on the bench top, as the warm food will encourage bacterial growth; this is especially important with casseroles and stews where food poisoning bacteria can actually survive the cooking process. Modern refrigerators can cope with small amounts of hot foods being placed directly into them; wait for the steam to stop rising from the food, then place, uncovered, in the refrigerator until cool. Once cool, cover the container or wrap the meat tightly with plastic wrap. Large amounts of food should be divided into smaller containers before cooling. If you do not expect to eat the food within two or three days, it is best to freeze it.

HOW LONG DO PRESERVED SALAMIS AND LUNCHEON MEATS KEEP FOR?

Ham, corned beef, polish salami and other luncheon meats available from delicatessens, must be stored in the refrigerator (however, do not allow them to come into contact with fresh meats). Pâtés should also be refrigerated.

Some fermented salamis, bacon and whole hams will keep for two to three weeks, while sliced luncheon meats will keep only for three or four days after purchase. It is a good idea to buy only small amounts of sliced luncheon meats.

Pre-packaged delicatessen items can be stored until the "best before" date. These are often vacuum packaged and have a longer shelf life, but any damaged or swollen packages should be avoided. A slight sour smell may be noticeable as the product starts to lose quality.

IS IT SAFE TO STORE PET FOOD IN THE SAME FRIDGE WE USE FOR THE FOOD WE EAT?

Meat designated as "pet food" should not come into direct contact with meat for human consumption as it may have been produced under less hygienic conditions. It should be well wrapped and stored in the coldest part of the refrigerator.

WHAT'S THE BEST WAY TO STORE RAW MEAT?

Raw meat should be kept separate from cooked food, and stored on the bottom shelf of the refrigerator to avoid juices dripping down and contaminating other food.

Always store raw meat in the coldest part of the refrigerator (usually the bottom shelf). Wrapped raw meat can be kept safely for up to three days, and unwrapped meat for up to five days at 0°C to 3°C.

Uncooked minced meat, liver and kidneys need careful storage because they carry large numbers of bacteria. Always store them in the coldest part of the refrigerator, as close as possible to 0°C for no more than three days.

Cured meat has a longer storage life than fresh meat. Unwrapped cured meat may last up to three weeks at 0°C to 3°C.

WHAT'S THE DIFFERENCE BETWEEN HOT-SMOKED AND COLD-SMOKED SALMON?

Both these forms have been around since before refrigeration. Hot smoking is a form of cooking whereby the smoke is circulated over the salmon for a short time at a high temperature, cooking the fish. This style of cooking results in a moist, subtly smoked salmon that flakes easily with a fork. It can be served cold or heated gently and stirred through pasta or salads.

Cold smoking is a method of curing food whereby smoke is circulated over the salmon at a low temperature for a relatively long period of time. The finished product is uncooked, leaving the texture unchanged. When a recipe askes for "smoked salmon", it is the thinly sliced, cold-smoked salmon that is used.

HOW DO I STORE RAW POULTRY?

Remove any plastic wrap around the raw poultry, then wash thoroughly and dry with paper towel; store in an adequately ventilated container in the coldest part of the refrigerator for two to three days.

Below is the storage life of some chilled foods in the coldest part of the refrigerator. Many of these are labelled with a "use-by-date", which can be used as a guide to the shelf life of the unopened product.

STORAGE TIMES

FOOD	EXPECTED SHELF LIFE IN THE REFRIGERATOR
Seafood	3 days
Crustaceans and molluscs	2 days
Meat	3-5 days
Minced meat and offal	2-3 days
Cured meat	2-3 weeks
Poultry	3 days
Fruit juices	7-14 days
Milk	5-7 days
Cream	5 days
Cheese	variable (1-3 months)
Soft cheeses e.g. camembert, brie	2-3 weeks
Cottage, ricotta, cream cheeses	10 days
Eggs	3-6 weeks
Butter	8 weeks
Margarine	variable (6 months)
Oil and fat	variable (6 months)

Food Science Australia

HOW DO I STORE FRESH FISH?

Fresh whole fish should be scaled, gutted and cleaned (your fishmonger should be able to do this for you). Rinse the cleaned fish under cold running water then pat dry with absorbent paper towel to remove any traces of scale or intestine. Place the fish in a covered container, or on a plate covered with plastic wrap, and store in the coldest part of the fridge for two to three days.

For fish fillets and cutlets, remove any wrapping or packaging and rinse under cold running water. Pat pieces dry, then place in a covered container, or on a plate covered with plastic wrap, and store in the coldest part of the fridge for two to three days.

WHAT'S THE BEST WAY TO STORE SHELLFISH?

Clean and rinse squid, cuttlefish and octopus, pat dry and store in the coldest part of the refrigerator, in a covered container, or on a plate or tray covered with plastic wrap. Use within two to three days.

Store prawns in a covered container, or on a plate or tray covered with plastic wrap, in the coldest part of the refrigerator. Use within two days.

Crustaceans, such as crabs and lobsters, can be bought live or cooked. Live crustaceans should be eaten as soon as possible after purchase. Keep in a cool place or in the coldest part of the refrigerator, covered with a very damp cloth, ensuring the cloth remains damp. Cooked crustaceans should be stored in the coldest part of the refrigerator, in a covered container, or on a plate or tray covered with plastic wrap. Use within two to three days.

Molluscs, such as mussels and oysters, must be bought live as they deteriorate rapidly. Place in a container, cover with a damp cloth and keep in the warmest part of the refrigerator, usually the crisper (5°C), ensuring the cloth remains damp, for up to three days. They can also be stored in the coldest part of the house away from sunlight; place in a large bowl and cover loosely with a damp cloth, or store in a damp hessian bag or in a bucket of cold salted water, covered with a damp cloth. Before cooking discard any shells that are open and don't close when tapped or gently squeezed.

LIVING A LONG WAY FROM THE FISH MARKETS, I LIKE TO BUY UP BIG WHEN I VISIT. WHAT'S THE BEST WAY TO FREEZE SEAFOOD?

While fresh seafood always tastes best, sometimes frozen is more practical. Just make sure the seafood you buy as fresh, hasn't already been defrosted by your fishmonger. Make sure you transport seafood, fresh or frozen, in a freezer bag and refrigerate or freeze it as soon as possible. Always defrost seafood in the refrigerator, not at room temperature.

Commercially frozen seafood is frozen very rapidly at lower temperatures than most domestic freezers can attain. This preserves the delicate texture of the flesh. If you must freeze seafood at home, it should be kept at -18°C.

Scale, gut and clean whole fish, then rinse under cold water and pat dry. Place whole fish, or fillets and cutlets, in an airtight freezer bag, extract as much air as possible; label and date. Whole non-oily fish can be frozen for up to six months; whole oily fish (tuna, salmon, sardines, mullet, etc) and all fish fillets, steaks and cutlets can be frozen for up to three months.

Gut and clean squid, cuttlefish and octopus. Place in an airtight freezer bag and extract as much air as possible; label and date. Freeze for up to three months.

Meat from molluscs (mussels, scallops, oysters) can be frozen for up to three months. Place in an airtight freezer bag and extract as much air as possible; label and date.

Crustaceans (crabs, lobsters, etc) can be frozen for up to three months. Wrap in foil then place in an airtight freezer bag; extract as much air as possible, label and date.

Place unshelled prawns in a plastic container and cover with water, then seal and freeze. This forms a large ice-block that insulates the prawns. Label, date and freeze for up to three months.

HOW DO I CHECK THE TEMPERATURE IN MY FRIDGE?

While the thermostat controls the temperature of your fridge, you will need a fridge thermometer (available from hardware and kitchenware stores) to check the actual temperature of your fridge. Put the thermometer in the coldest part of the fridge (usually the bottom two shelves); leave it overnight and check it in the morning. If the temperature is higher than 5°C, adjust the thermostat and check the temperature again in four hours.

SOME OF THE FOOD IN MY FRIDGE SEEMS TO GO OFF QUICKLY. HOW COLD SHOULD MY FRIDGE BE TO SAFELY STORE FOOD?

Ideally, you want the main compartment of your fridge to be between 0°C and 5°C; the freezer compartment should be between -15°C and -18°C.

WHAT IS FREEZER BURN?

Freezer burn occurs when foods have been exposed to air during freezing causing the surface to lose moisture, and making it appear dry and discoloured. You can still eat food that has been affected by freezer burn, however, it is more likely to have off flavours and a tough, chewy texture.

CAN I FREEZE FOOD INDEFINITELY?

All foods that have been frozen have a use-by-date; these recommended freezing times ensure the food maintains its texture and flavour. Foods that are frozen for too long can lose moisture and become dry and tough. Depending on the type of food, most can be safely frozen between 1-12 months if it has been correctly packed and frozen at -15°C to -18°C. These days, many refrigerators come with a manufacturer's note on freezing times for certain foods.

REFRIGERATION HINTS

Locate your refrigerator in an area with adequate air space to allow it to operate effectively. Your instruction booklet will outline the clearances required. Avoid locating the refrigerator in very hot places such as next to an oven or dishwasher.

Use a refrigerator thermometer and keep the door of the refrigerator open for the shortest possible time.

Defrost the refrigerator regularly. Ice build up reduces the operation efficiency. This does not apply to automatic defrost models. Door seals should also be checked regularly.

Throw out food that is going off. Putting it in a colder part of the refrigerator will not stop it deteriorating further.

Store food you want to keep for a long time, or items like seafood that are quite susceptible to spoilage, in the coldest part of the refrigerator. Cover all cooked foods and, when practical, store them on a shelf above uncooked foods. This minimises the risk of food poisoning organisms being transferred from uncooked to cooked food through drips.

Foods with strong odours, such as seafood and some cheeses, should be wrapped, and you should avoid storing them for long periods near foods such as eggs, milk and cream, which are susceptible to tainting.

Some flexible films are effective barriers to the transmission of odours, but they are not readily available to consumers. The common cling wrap polyethylene and PVC films are not very effective barriers, but they are useful in the short term and stop spillages. Closed glass or plastic containers are preferable to wrapping in plastic wrap.

The "best-before" date is your best guide to storage life of a particular perishable food. However, it is only useful if the food has been stored correctly before you buy it. Observe the food storage practices in your favourite stores and, if you see food mishandled, shop elsewhere.

Food Science Australia

MY PACKET OF SPLIT PEAS DOESN'T HAVE A USE-BY-DATE. HOW LONG DO DRIED FOODS KEEP FOR?

Dehydrated or dried foods tend to have a long storage life if stored in a cool dark place away from obvious sources of heat, such as a stove or direct sunlight, and can often last many months or years. However, they do deteriorate slowly over time and can develop discolouration, off-flavours, become lumpy and won't soften when cooked, remaining hard and unpalatable. High temperatures and exposure to air (particularly humid air) hasten these changes.

Use-by-dates apply to the unopened container stored in cool, dry conditions. Once opened, the recommended storage time no longer applies. Dried foods will keep in an unopened container for about six months at 21°C to 24°C.

Store any unused portion in a screw-top jar, sealable metal container, or rigid, airtight plastic container similar in size to the amount being stored (large air spaces also encourage deterioration). Storing these foods in the refrigerator may also increase storage life.

I'M ALWAYS FINDING WEEVILS IN MY DRIED FOODS. WE LIVE IN A HUMID CLIMATE – COULD THIS BE THE CAUSE?

Unfortunately, insect infestation can be a big problem with dry foods, and this is a good reason why you shouldn't buy and store large quantities of dried foods at home. Eggs laid in the food by insects before the food is packaged may survive fumigation treatments, and can hatch under warm and moist conditions, such as in humid climates. Insects also may get into dried foods by chewing through the packaging or by entering after the package has been opened.

Store dried foods in airtight rigid containers with screw tops or other secure lids, whether opened or not. This will ensure that any insects in the food do not contaminate other packages. It also makes disposal of infested material simple. Also store in a cool place away from obvious sources of heat, such as the stove or direct sunlight. Regular inspection of dried foods, at least once a fortnight in warm weather, is also recommended.

WHAT'S THE DIFFERENCE BETWEEN "USE-BY-DATES", "BEST-BEFORE" DATES AND "BAKED-ON" DATES?

"Use-by-dates" indicate the end of acceptable storage life. Foods that should be consumed before a certain date because of safety reasons must be marked with a use-by-date, and should not be consumed once this date is past. It is illegal for shops to sell products after this date has expired.

The "best-before" date signifies that the product may have lost some of its quality, but it should still retain its colour, taste, texture and flavour as long as it has been stored correctly. Products may still be sold after the best-before date has expired.

Items with a shelf life of fewer than seven days, such as bread, may include a "baked-on" or "baked-for" date instead of a best-before date.

HOW DO I STORE PRESERVES?

Preserves cover a wide range of food: it includes bottled fruit, jams, jellies, pickles, chutney and pastes, etc. Store preserves in a cool, dark, dry place until required. If you live in a humid climate, the best storage place is the refrigerator. Once opened, all preserves must be kept, covered, in the refrigerator.

HOW DO I STORE RELISHES?

Relishes should always be stored in the fridge, and kept for two or three weeks only, regardless of whether they are opened or unopened.

SHOULD FRUIT AND VEGETABLES ALWAYS BE REFRIGERATED?

No, some produce, particularly those from the tropics, such as pineapple, bananas and sweet potatoes, are cold sensitive and should not be stored in the refrigerator. However, most fresh produce is heat sensitive and should be stored in the coolest part of the house, or refrigerated, as necessary.

Rockmelon, pineapple, papaya, bananas, mangoes, avocados, stone fruit and pears need to be ripened at room temperature. They can then be refrigerated for a short time only.

SOME OF MY VEGETABLES AND FRUIT SEEM TO WILT RAPIDLY WHEN I PUT THEM IN THE FRIDGE. HOW DO I STOP THIS?

Not all vegetables and fruit need to be kept in the fridge; some are cold sensitive, others can lose much of their moisture. If fruit and vegetables are to be refrigerated, cool them first in the refrigerator, then place into paper bags or perforated plastic bags; this reduces sweating and moisture loss.

Keep leafy and root vegetables, including silver beet, broccoli, carrots and parsnips, in perforated plastic bags, to reduce shrivelling or wilting due to water loss. By removing leafy tops from carrots, parsnips, turnips and beetroot, their storage life can be extended by   weeks in the refrigerator.

Some fruits and vegetables, such as citrus fruits, passionfruit, cucumbers, capsicums and eggplants, lose their moisture once refrigerated and start to wilt; wrapping them in plastic wrap will help prevent this.

HOW DO I STORE POTATOES TO STOP THEM FROM SPROUTING?

Keep potatoes in a cool, dark, well-ventilated place to avoid "greening" and sprouting; remove from plastic bags and place in a strong paper bag or box or in a wire or plastic bin. Potatoes will eventually sprout, so use them within three to four weeks.

SHOPPING TIPS

Buy good quality food if you're going to store it for any length of time. If you buy food that is marked down, make sure you use it immediately, or store it in the freezer. Food bargains are usually close to the end of their use-by-date, so are not always of high quality and may spoil rapidly.

Only buy fish and shellfish, fresh and cured meats, dairy products and prepared foods (such as salads, quiches, filled cakes and other ready-made meals) from the refrigerated or frozen section of the supermarket.

Don't buy swollen chilled food packages as the contents are spoiling. While chilled juices, unprocessed cheeses, yogurt and fresh pastas all contain harmless microbes when packaged, swelling is a sign that microbes have been allowed to grow and produce gas. This usually means the products have been stored at warm temperatures for some time or that they are near the end of their shelf life.

Examine chilled products packed in transparent wraps or containers for mould growth. Some moulds are able to grow at refrigeration temperatures.

Take an insulated cooler bag or icepacks with you when you go shopping, and always buy refrigerated food last. Never leave chilled foods sitting in the car – they should be placed in the refrigerator or freezer as soon as possible.

Avoid overbuying refrigerated foods unless you are going to freeze them; chilled foods are perishable and have only a limited shelf life.

Food Science Australia

Optimum storage conditions and approximate storage life for fresh fruit and vegetables in the home.

SHELF LIFE	COLDEST PART OF REFRIGERATOR
Very short self life (often less than 1 week)	Apricots, Asparagus, Avocados (ripe), Blackberries, Cherries, Custard apples (ripe), Figs, Green peas, Guavas, Herbs (most types), Honeydew (cut), Leafy vegetables, Loquats, Lychees, Mushrooms, Nectarines (ripe), Peaches, Pears (ripe), Persimmons (ripe), Plums (juicy/ripe), Raspberries, Rockmelon (cut), Shallots, Spring onions, Strawberries, Watermelon (cut)
Short shelf life (1 week)	Blueberries, Broccoli, Chestnuts, Grapes, Lettuce, Passionfruit, Plums (dry/unripe), Red radish (topped), Rhubarb, Sweet corn
Medium shelf life (2 weeks)	Apples – most varieties, Brussels sprouts, Cabbage (cut), Carrots (topped), Celery, Daikon Kohlrabi, Pears (unripe), Persimmons (unripe), Turnips
Longer shelf life (3-4 weeks)	Apples (Granny Smith and Fuji) Beetroot (topped), Cabbage (whole), Parsnips, Quinces, Wombok

Food Science Australia

WARMEST PART OF REFRIGERATOR	IN A COOL PLACE IN THE HOME
Papaya (ripe)	Bananas (ripe) Basil (stems in water) Custard apples (unripe) Mangoes (unripe) Nectarines (unripe) Papaya (unripe) Peaches (unripe) Pumpkin (immature) Rambutan Rockmelon (whole) Squash (immature) Starfruit
Capsicum, Chilli, Green beans, Mangoes (ripe), Pumpkin (cut)	Bananas (green) Cucumber Eggplant Lettuce (hydroponic) Pineapple Tomatoes Watermelon (whole) Zucchini
Grapefruit, Lemons, Limes, Mandarins, Oranges	Avocados (firm)
	Garlic Lemon grass Honeydew (whole) Kumara Onions Potatoes (in the dark) Pumpkin (mature, whole) Squash (mature, whole)

MEASUREMENTS

Get the best out of your oven

How to measure wet & dry ingredients

American measurements

Oven temperatures

Often-used ingredient measurements

I HAVE JUST GOT A NEW OVEN. DO YOU HAVE ANY TIPS TO ENSURE WHAT I COOK IS PERFECT?

It's important you get to know your oven – particularly when it comes to baking cakes, biscuits and slices.

If you are using a fan-forced oven, check the operating instructions for best results. As a general rule, reduce the temperature by 10°C to 20°C when using the fan during baking; recipes might also take slightly less time to bake than specified in recipes. Some ovens give better results if the fan is used for only part of the baking time; in this case, it is usually best to introduce the fan during the last half of the baking time.

Before you preheat the oven, position the oven racks – they expand when they're hot, and can be quite difficult to move. Also, check that the cake pans you're using fit on the rack properly, allowing space for the cake, etc., to rise. It's always easier to remove baked goods from the "top" rack in the oven, than from between the racks.

If you often bake more than two batches of slices or biscuits, buy another oven rack or two, as fan-forced ovens should bake four racks of biscuits, etc., evenly.

Best results are obtained by baking in an oven preheated to the required temperature; this takes about 10 minutes. Be sure to check the preheating instructions; some ovens have a particular preheating mode, and some don't. Make sure you choose the correct mode needed for whatever you're baking.

MY OVEN, DESPITE HAVING A FAN, BROWNS UNEVENLY. WHAT CAN I DO TO CORRECT THIS?

Some domestic fan-forced ovens do have "hot spots" – this is why it's important to get to know your oven. Do whatever it takes to get even browning and baking. Rotate or turn the pans, or move them from one shelf to another. If the baking time is short – up to 30 minutes, change the positions of the pans halfway through the baking time. For longer baking times, make the changes every 20 to 30 minutes.

WHAT IS THE CORRECT WAY TO MEASURE LIQUIDS AND DRY INGREDIENTS SUCH AS FLOUR AND SUGAR WHEN COOKING?

Liquids should be measured in a marked jug; stand it on a flat surface, then check it at eye level for accuracy. Spoon and cup measurements should be levelled off with a knife or spatula. When measuring ingredients such as honey or syrup warm the cup or spoon in hot water then dry it completely before pouring in the honey or syrup.

ARE AMERICAN CUPS AND SPOON MEASURES THE SAME AS OURS?

The difference between an American and an Australian measuring cup is so small (less than a tablespoon) it's irrelevant. It's important to note that Australia is the only country in the world that has a 20ml tablespoon measure, the rest are 15ml.
1 American cup = 237 ml (Australia = 250ml)
1 American tablespoon = 15ml (Australia = 20ml)
1 American teaspoon = 5ml (same as Australia).

I HAVE AN OLD RECIPE THAT CALLS FOR 1 GILL OF MILK – HOW MUCH IS A GILL?

The three main measurement systems in use around the world today are the U.S. Customary system, the (British) Imperial system and the (International) metric system. A gill is a liquid measure: in the U.S. Customary system it's equal to 4 fluid ounces or a ¼ pint – which roughly equals 125ml in our (metric) measures. However, in the British Imperial system, 1 gill equals 5 fluid ounces (about 150ml).

The Imperial pint is 20 fluid ounces (or 600ml in the metric system) and the U.S. Customary pint is 16 fluid ounces (or 500ml in the metric system).

These oven temperatures are only a guide for conventional ovens. For fan-forced ovens, check the manufacturer's manual.

OVEN TEMPERATURES

	°C (CELSIUS)	°F (FAHRENHEIT)	GAS MARK
Very slow	120	250	½
Slow	150	275-300	1-2
Moderately slow	160	325	3
Moderate	180	350-375	4-5
Moderately hot	200	400	6
Hot	220	425-450	7-8
Very hot	240	475	9

LIQUID MEASURES

METRIC	IMPERIAL
30ml	1 fluid oz
60ml	2 fluid oz
100ml	3 fluid oz
125ml	4 fluid oz
150ml	5 fluid oz (¼ pint/1 gill)
190ml	6 fluid oz
250ml	8 fluid oz
300ml	10 fluid oz (½ pint)
500ml	16 fluid oz
600ml	20 fluid oz (1 pint)
1000ml (1 litre)	1¾ pints

DRY MEASURES	
METRIC	IMPERIAL
15g	½oz
30g	1oz
60g	2oz
90g	3oz
125g	4oz (¼lb)
155g	5oz
185g	6oz
220g	7oz
250g	8oz (½lb)
280g	9oz
315g	10oz
345g	11oz
375g	12oz (¾lb)
410g	13oz
440g	14oz
470g	15oz
500g	16oz (1lb)
750g	24oz (1½lb)
1kg	32oz (2lb)

LENGTH MEASURES	
METRIC	IMPERIAL
3mm	⅛in
6mm	¼in
1cm	½in
2cm	¾in
2.5cm	1in
5cm	2in
6cm	2½in
8cm	3in
10cm	4in
13cm	5in
15cm	6in
18cm	7in
20cm	8in
23cm	9in
25cm	10in
28cm	11in
30cm	12in (1ft)

SINGLE CUP MEASUREMENTS

Almonds		Chocolate	
Coarsely chopped	160g	Coarsely chopped	175g
Finely chopped	150g	Finely chopped	180g
Flaked	80g	Grated	100g
Meal (ground)	120g	Choc Bits	190g
Slivered	140g	Choc Melts	150g
Whole (blanched)	160g	**Chutney**	320g
Apples		**Cocoa**	100g
Dried, coarsely chopped	60g	**Coconut**	
Canned pie	225g	Desiccated	80g
Apricots		Flaked	50g
Dried halves	150g	Milk powder	100g
Coarsely chopped dried	150g	Shredded	75g
Chopped glacé	250g	**Corn flakes**	40g
Canned pie	250g	**Cornmeal**	170g
Arrowroot	150g	**Couscous**	200g
Barley	200g	**Cranberries** (dried)	130g
Beans/peas (dried)	200g	**Crème fraîche**	240g
Berries (frozen, mixed)	150g	**Currants** (dried)	160g
Bran		**Curry paste**	300g
All-Bran	70g	**Custard powder**	125g
Flakes	60g	**Dates** (seeded, dried)	140g
Oat Bran	120g	Coarsely chopped	140g
Unprocessed	120g	**Flour**	
Brazil nuts (whole)	160g	Plain, self-raising (S-R)	150g
Breadcrumbs		Wholemeal plain, S-R	160g
Fresh, stale	70g	Bread	160g
Packaged	100g	Buckwheat	150g
Burghul	160g	Chickpea (besan)	150g
Cashews (whole)	150g	Cornflour	150g
Cheese		Gluten-free (plain + S-R)	135g
Cheddar,		Lentil	150g
grated coarsely	120g	Maize	180g
Cottage	200g	Oatmeal	
Mascarpone	250g	(fine or medium grind)	140g
Mozzarella,		Potato	150g
grated coarsely	100g	Rice	200g
Parmesan, flaked	80g	Rye	125g
Parmesan, grated finely	80g	Semolina	180g
Ricotta	240g	Soya	125g
Cherries		**Ginger**	
Glacé, whole	200g	Glacé	230g
Stoneless		Pickled pink	280g
(canned, drained)	200g	Crystallised	220g

SINGLE CUP MEASUREMENTS (continued)

Glucose, liquid	350g	**Prunes** (with seeds)	180g
Golden syrup	350g	Seeded	170g
Hazelnuts (whole)	140g	**Quinoa flakes**	200g
Meal (ground)	100g	**Raisins**	180g
Honey	360g	**Relish**	280g
Jam	320g	**Rhubarb**	
Lentils	200g	Chopped coarsely	110g
Macadamias (whole)	140g	**Rice**	200g
Ground	120g	**Rice Bubbles**	35g
Marmalade	340g	**Rolled oats**	90g
Mayonnaise	300g	**Sago**	200g
Milk powder	100g	**Semolina**	160g
Millet	200g	**Sour cream**	240g
Mixed dried fruit	160g	**Sugar**	
Mixed peel	170g	White	220g
Molasses	370g	Raw	220g
Muesli		Demerara	220g
Natural	110g	Brown, firmly packed	220g
Toasted	130g	Icing sugar	160g
Nuts (crushed)	140g	Palm sugar	270g
Olives	160g	**Sultanas**	160g
Seeded	120g	**Tomato**	
Pasta		Paste	280g
Risoni	220g	Puree	280g
Macaroni (small)	180g	Pasta sauce	260g
Peaches		Semi-dried in oil, drained	150g
Dried halves	150g	Sun-dried in oil, drained	150g
Coarsely chopped dried	150g	Sun-dried without oil	60g
Finely chopped dried	160g	**Treacle**	360g
Whole glacé	250g	**Walnuts** (whole)	100g
Chopped glacé	250g	Ground	120g
Canned pie	240g	**Wheat Germ**	100g
Chopped drained	260g	**Yogurt**	280g
Peanuts (whole)	140g		
Crushed	140g		
Peanut butter	280g		
Pecans (whole)	120g		
Ground	110g		
Pine Nuts	155g		
Pistachios			
In Shell	175g		
Shelled	140g		
Ground	130g		
Polenta	170g		

INDEX

ACP BOOKS
General manager Christine Whiston
Editorial director Susan Tomnay
Creative director & designer Hieu Chi Nguyen
Senior editor Wendy Bryant
Text Kitchen food director Pamela Clark
Director of sales Brian Cearnes
Marketing manager Bridget Cody
Senior business analyst Rebecca Varela
Operations manager David Scotto
Production manager Victoria Jefferys
International rights enquiries Laura Bamford
lbamford@acpuk.com

ACP Books are published by ACP Magazines a division of PBL Media Pty Limited
Publishing director, Women's lifestyle Pat Ingram
Director of sales, Women's lifestyle Lynette Phillips
Commercial manager, Women's lifestyle Seymour Cohen
Marketing director, Women's lifestyle Matthew Dominello
Public relations manager, Women's lifestyle Hannah Deveraux
Research director, Women's lifestyle Justin Stone
PBL Media, Chief Executive Officer Ian Law

Produced by ACP Books, Sydney.

Published by ACP Books, a division of ACP Magazines Ltd,
54 Park St, Sydney; GPO Box 4088, Sydney, NSW 2001.
phone (02) 9282 8618; fax (02) 9267 9438.
acpbooks@acpmagazines.com.au; www.acpbooks.com.au

Printed by Everbest Printing Co. Ltd, China

Australia Distributed by Network Services, phone +61 2 9282 8777; fax +61 2 9264 3278;
networkweb@networkservicescompany.com.au
United Kingdom Distributed by Australian Consolidated Press (UK),
phone (01604) 642 200; fax (01604) 642 300; books@acpuk.com
New Zealand Distributed by Southern Publishers Group, 21 Newton Rd, Newton, Auckland.
phone (64 9) 360 0692; fax (64 9) 360 0695; hub@spg.co.nz
South Africa Distributed by PSD Promotions,
phone (27 11) 392 6065/6/7; fax (27 11) 392 6079/80; orders@psdprom.co.za
Canada Distributed by Publishers Group Canada
phone (800) 663 5714; fax (800) 565 3770; service@raincoast.com

Title: Ask Pamela Q&A / compiler, Pamela Clark.
ISBN 978 1 86396 871 3 (pbk)
Notes: Includes index.
Subjects: Cookery – Miscellanea.
Other Authors/Contributors: Clark, Pamela.
Dewey Number: 641.5
© ACP Magazines Ltd 2009
ABN 18 053 273 546

To order books, phone 136 116 (within Australia).
Send recipe enquiries to: recipeenquiries@acpmagazines.com.au